A HISTORICAL NARRATIVE OF
IMAM HUSAYN IBN ALI

HUSAYN
THE SAGA OF HOPE

JALAL MOUGHANIA

THE
MAINSTAY
FOUNDATION

Husayn: The Saga of Hope

Author: Jalal Moughania

© 2022 The Mainstay Foundation

Calligraphy cover design: Zuhayr Husayni

Printed in the United States.

ISBN: 978-1943393206

To Imam Husayn's brother and partner in vision...
Imam Hasan ibn Ali

Peace be upon Husayn

And upon Ali ibn Husayn

And upon the children of Husayn

And upon the companions of Husayn

The champions that gave their lives

And pledged to never leave

Their beloved Husayn

CONTENTS

NOTES ON USAGE, SPELLING AND FORMATTING

In writing this book, I have elected to use more familiar English spellings for names of figures and subjects and have done so without diacritical marks. Thus, you will see Ali instead of 'Ali and Umar instead of 'Umar.

In addition, for the sake of fluidity, I have limited the use of honorary titles for the Holy Prophet Muhammad and his Household, such as Imam Husayn and Lady Zaynab, peace be upon them all. Therefore, you will see that most of the text will refer to them simply by their first name: Hasan, Husayn, Zaynab, etc.

I have also limited the use of their full names, such as Ali ibn Abi Talib and Fatima bint Muhammad, to avoid the "Russian novel effect," keeping in mind the English reader who may be more easily confused with multiple unfamiliar names. There are times that the full names, or the second part of the names, are used to either distinguish between personalities with similar names, such as Abdullah ibn Abbas and Abdullah ibn Umar in the same conversation. They may also be used at times to emphasize the individual's parentage or lineage.

Furthermore, though "Koran" is often used in English works, I have elected to use the more proper spelling of "Quran" to differentiate between the *qaf* and *kaf* in the Arabic, which, if confused, could render different meanings of the word.

The reader should note that the supplication of *salawat* (a prayer asking God to send His peace and blessings upon Muhammad and the household of Muhammad) and salutations (peace be upon them) are usually recited at the mention of the Holy Prophet and his family. This is normally marked in elaborate calligraphy in Arabic text, or with (s), (a), or a similar mark in English text. Such marks do not appear in this book, so as not to disturb the flow of the reader. Nonetheless, the reader is encouraged to recite such prayers in their honor for the blessings of their mentioning.

It is worthy of note that I also relied on the English translation of Ali Quli Qara'i when citing the verses of the Holy Quran throughout this book, with minor adaptations. Moreover, I have italicized Arabic words, other than the names of individuals, when they first appear in the book.

In translating dialogue, I opted for utilizing an idiomizing translation (see: Dickins, Hervey, and Higgins, Thinking Arabic Translation, p. 15 (2nd Edition, 2017)). Thus, I opted at times to sacrifice some equivalency and detail in the translation, in favor of providing a more natural and flowing text.

Moreover, while I attempted to be as faithful as possible to the information provided in the sources I relied on, this book does contain some natural dramatization of the subject historical events, without straying from the historical accounts. For example, the reader will see that some characters are portrayed as 'smiling' or 'crying,' even though some particular historical accounts may not mention their emotional state or the particularity of 'smiling' or 'crying.' Without these minor expressions and/or dramatizations, it may be difficult for the common reader to fully appreciate the historical narrative and understand its emotional context.

I would also like to make a few notes regarding formatting, particularly the formatting of dialogue in this book. There is a lot of dialogue in this narrative, intentionally delivered as such to give the reader the experience of witnessing the conversations that shaped such events in history. For parts of quoted content that is in the form of a sermon, monologues, lengthy prayers, or letters, the words of the speaker appear in the form of an indented and italicized block quote. Short quotes, such as those recalled from the Prophet about Ali or Husayn, are also shown in this particular format with the intention of emphasis.

The paragraphs of quoted dialogue are indented, otherwise all other paragraphs do not have indentation with the absence of dialogue in said paragraphs to distinguish between dialogue and non-dialogue text.

I pray that these choices make the book more reader friendly to the intended audience, the English-speaking reader.

Any mistakes or shortcomings are mine alone.

PREFACE

In a distant age and climate, the tragic scene of the death of Husayn will awaken the sympathy of the coldest reader.

– Edward Gibbon, The Decline and Fall of the Roman Empire

In 680 AD, on the plains of Karbala, Iraq, the grandson of Islam's Prophet Muhammad, Husayn ibn Ali, was brutally slaughtered by an army of thirty-thousand men at the order of the Umayyad caliph Yazid ibn Muawiya. History tells us that when presented with other options, such as to retreat to Yemen or other faraway lands, Husayn refused and insisted on continuing his journey for Iraq. Husayn knew of his inevitable fate and embraced it – that he would be killed by an unjust lot and in a land that would forever be enshrined in the hearts of men and women across the ages, as Karbala.

While Husayn was killed at the whims of men's greed and lust for power, what did Husayn actually die for? What was the purpose of his most tragic death? Even beyond the stance of justice against injustice and the notion of supporting the oppressed against oppression, all of which are noble pursuits of humanity, the foundational purpose for which Husayn died is very simple.

Husayn died for the same thing that he lived for. In fact, he lived and died for the same purpose that his brother, his mother and father, and his grandfather lived and died for – Islam.

Husayn lived and died for the religion of God, the faith of his grandfather Muhammad, and the creed by which his mother Fatima and father Ali raised their loyal companions on. It was that creed, that faith, that religion, for which Husayn would give everything. And it is his story, his saga of hope, that continues to bring life to the faith that billions of people have followed for centuries.

This book is about that story. It tells the tale of Husayn's amazing life and most heroic death. Husayn grew up in the lap of his grandfather, the Prophet of Islam, and was slain at the hands of the same people who claimed to follow his grandfather. Husayn was by far the greatest leader, most noble warrior, and highest scholar of his time. He is certainly one of the most inspiring and consequential figures in human history. His legacy of sacrifice, love, and hope have moved even the coldest of hearts, perhaps even those who took part in killing him.

Little can be said without falling short of the glory that was and always will be Husayn ibn Ali. Within Islamic tradition, no other *Imam* (divinely appointed leader) had the honor of being the son of an Imam, the brother of an Imam, and the father of an Imam. Husayn was the son of the Commander of the Faithful, Ali ibn Abi Talib (the first Imam). He was the younger brother of Imam Hasan ibn Ali (the second Imam). He was the father of the young man who survived the Massacre of Karbala, Imam Ali ibn Husayn (the fourth Imam). That honor was for Husayn alone. And though every member of the *Ahlulbayt* (the Prophet's household) would be a beacon of light in their own right, Husayn would forever be the ship of salvation and the light of guidance whom the Prophet promised. Prophet Muhammad would say, "Husayn is the ship of salvation and the light of guidance."

> *His love was the Prophet's love, and to love the Prophet was to love God. The Prophet made this an essential part of Muslim ethos and identity. Loving Husayn was inevitable. He told his companions, "Husayn is of me and I am of him, God loves whoever loves Husayn."*

I present this book as a humble contribution in the spirit of Imam Husayn's legacy, within the growing body of English literature that studies and brings light to this history and heritage. The intention behind this modest offering is to help provide the English reader a more comprehensive narrative of Husayn's life, especially his last days, that culminated with the Massacre of Karbala. I pray that through this book the reader will better understand the circumstances surrounding Ashura, how Husayn's sacrifice came to be, and what happened both before and after the ultimate tragedy that was his killing.

In providing a background of the development of this work, I invite the reader to make note of a few important things regarding my research. For one, it is worthy to note the sources used to inform this narrative presented for the reader. The primary historical sources I referred to, in the content before and after the Day of Ashura, were Shaykh al-Tabari's (839 AD – 923 AD) *Tarikh al-Rusul wa al-Muluk* – and Shaykh al-Mufid's (948 AD – 1022 AD) *Kitab Al-Irshad*. A very useful secondary source that I benefited from in my research, which helped guide me to some of the primary references used, was the book of Allamah Baqir al-Qureshi titled, *The Life of Imam Husayn: Research and Analysis*. For the detailed accounts presented on the Day of Ashura, a most beneficial resource was Mohamed Ali Al-Bodairi's *The Saga: The Battle of Karbala*, published by the Mainstay Foundation in 2018. This encyclopedia relied most heavily and pointed me to some of the classical sources such as Abu Mikhnaf's (689 AD – 775 AD) *Maqtal al-Husayn* and al-Muwaffaq al-Khowarizmi's (1091 AD – 1172 AD) *Maqtal al-Husayn*. In addition, some more contemporary works from the 20th century relied on here were Sayyid Abd al-Razzaq al-Muqarram's (1898 AD – 1971 AD) *Maqtal al-Husayn*, Sayyid Muhsin al-Ameen's (1867 AD – 1952 AD) *Lawa'ij al-Ashjan* and Dr. Labeeb Beydoun's (b. 1938 AD) *Mawsu'at Karbala*, amongst others shared in the bibliography.

Furthermore, the reading of this normative period of Islamic history, and the presentation of this historical narrative, is primarily based on the writings and analysis of Grand Ayatollah M.S. Al-Hakeem's *Faji'at al-Taf (trans. Understanding Karbala)*, Ayatollah Shaykh Mahdi Chamseddine's *Thawrat al-Husayn (trans. Hussain's Revolution)*, and Ayatollah Shaykh Raadi Al-Yasine's *Sulh al-Hasan (trans. The Peace Treaty of al-Hasan)*. One of the common themes presented in these works is the understanding that the Prophet Muhammad and his family, as the vicegerents of God, acted on the basis of two principles: *hifdh al-din* (preservation of faith) and *hifdh al-dima'* (preservation of life). Their objective was to save and preserve Islam, as its guardians, and at the same time protect the sanctity of life and honor humanity. These works heavily contributed to my own understanding and reading of this time in history, especially when it came to the choices made by the Holy Prophet's household. For a more detailed list of sources used, I invite the reader to review the "Select Bibliography" found at the end of the book.

It is worthy to note that there are indeed other readings of history, particularly the events building up to the Tragedy of Ashura (i.e. the peace accord of Imam Hasan ibn Ali and Muawiya, the complexities of Kufan support for Muslim ibn Aqeel and Imam Husayn, the dynamics between Yazid ibn Muawiya and Ubaydallah ibn Ziyad, etc.). An example of a contemporary work with a new and/or different reading of some parts of the traditional narrative in this history is Ayatollah Sayyid Sami al-Badri's *Sulh al-Imam al-Hasan: Qiraa'a Jadeeda (trans. The Treaty of al-Hasan: A New Reading)*. While the different readings of this historical period are fascinating and enticing, I have chosen for this historical narrative, however, to relay the more common and traditional reading of history (as I understand them from the works of the scholars I formerly mentioned above). This, of course, is done without eliminating the possibility that other readings of these historical events exist, and such readings are a matter of scholarly discourse amongst historians of Islamic history. Nevertheless, the reader is invited to research these areas further and continue to keep an open mind when learning about the history of this foundational period of Islamic history and heritage.

I have written this work with no claim to scholarship or expertise in history or Islam. I am not a historian nor am I scholar of the faith. I am merely an aspiring student, with a keen interest in sharing what I am learning of history and religion. More specifically, I wish to share what I have learned with my fellow English readers, who may not have access to the traditional texts of Islamic history for one. And more importantly, they may not have been afforded a book that provides a historical narrative written for them, the English reader, in mind. As a number of notable translations of original works do exist, some of which I have greatly benefited from in addition to consulting the original texts, many translations do not resonate with English readers. The reason for this could be the staleness in some of the translations, that wish to stay true to the original text and fear straying from its original meanings. Thus, some translations may seem more literal and not translate the cultural meanings or understandings of what is intended. This work does not intend to replace those notable works, but merely to add to the overall benefit of this readership.

It is important to note that the objective of this work is not to provide an analysis of the different readings of history and interpretations of these events. Instead, the primary objective of this work is to deliver a holistic narrative or story-telling of the life and death of Imam Husayn ibn Ali, with a detailed focus on the last year of his life. This book, again, has been written and designed with the English reader in mind. Though the first to benefit from this work would reasonably be assumed to be the generally informed Shi'a Muslim, who has heard parts of the story of Imam Husayn's life and death through the commemorative gatherings held annually (*majalis*) in Muslim communities across the world. Still, this book is written with the hopes of a broader benefit in mind – to both informed and uninformed readers, whether they are Shi'a, non-Shi'a, Muslim, or non-Muslim.

The reader will find very specific details in the narrative of Imam Husayn's life, especially in his final days on the plains of Karbala. Much of these specific accounts, preserved in the books of Islamic history by scholars of Islam, can be attributed to the narrations relayed by three primary groups of people. One, there were bystanders who watched the battle of Karbala take place and did not participate in either camp who relayed much of what took place on that day. Two, the soldiers in the camp of Umar ibn Saad shared details of the battle. Three, the survivors of the massacre at Karbala from Husayn's family told the story of what they witnessed in vivid detail. One of the survivors on that day included Hasan II (or Hasan al-Muthanna) who participated in the battle and was severely injured, but managed to escape before being killed by the Umayyads. Another survivor and the successor of his father Imam Husayn, was Imam Ali ibn Husayn (also known as Zayn al-Abideen). Ali ibn Husayn was ill when the battle took place. It is said that he, along with Hasan II, were not killed due to the intercession of their aunt, Lady Zaynab, who stood before the enemy soldiers preventing them for taking any steps further. Lady Zaynab bint Ali was herself a survivor of the massacre, who would go on to be the greatest advocate of Husayn and the teller of his tragedy. Some of the survivors from the Day of Ashura included Husayn's sister Umm Kulthum, his daughters Fatima, Sukayna, Ruqayya, and even his grandson

Muhammad al-Baqir (the fifth Imam). This is in addition to the widows of Husayn's fallen companions who had accompanied them, as well as the rest of the women and children in the caravan from Husayn's family.

In reading this narrative, it is important to keep in mind a few additional matters. One, some parts of the story may seem 'unbelievable' or 'impractical' to the modern reader without understanding the context of these historical events as well as the customs and etiquettes of the Arabs of that time period (7th century), especially in war and battle.

For example, even with the presence of thousands of soldiers in battling camps, it was most common for duals or one-on-one skirmishes to take place. The best of one camp would come forward to challenge the best of the opposing camp. That was the standard and one of the most basic traditions of battle. That is why the reader will see the majority of the battle take place in this fashion, whereby the soldiers of Husayn would seek his permission one at a time before they entered the battlefield. There were times throughout the battle, in which Umar ibn Saad and his men would get fed up with the continuous losses they suffered in such duels. Thus, they would break this etiquette of war and ambush Husayn's men, either with cavalry or a wave of arrows by their archers. In fact, this took place even in the very beginning of the fight when Umar ibn Saad's camp grew tired of listening to Husayn's warnings against commencing battle altogether.

Without having this background and context, the reader may question why did the soldiers of Husayn go out one at a time for most of the battle and how did they have the opportunity for so much dialogue and going back and forth? Wouldn't it have been much more realistic that the evil army led by Umar ibn Saad would have simply run down the camp of Husayn and been done with it all ever so quickly? Why the continuous toing and froing? The reality was that the situation was quite complex. The individuals involved were complex. Yes, the Umayyad army came to commit the gravest crime in Muslim history, let alone human history. However, there were a variety of ambitions, hesitations, and motivations on the Day of Ashura amongst the camp of Umar ibn Saad.

One of the most intriguing, yet tragic, things about the Battle of Karbala, was the very challenge of Umar ibn Saad's army of the most basic etiquettes. Hence, the reader will see the same characters would break a custom and then follow it shortly later out of a sense of guilt or remorse; then moments later, would break it once again. Umar ibn Saad himself was reluctant to actually engage in battle against Husayn, until it was clearly ordered by Ubaydallah ibn Ziyad that there was no other way around it, as the reader will see in chapter nine and ten, for example. Umar ibn Saad was not innocent. He was motivated by the reward of ruling over a province in Iran that was promised to him by the governor. He just did not like the idea of having Husayn's blood on his hands. Was he willing to do other injustices? Absolutely. Did he eventually lead the army into battle against Husayn? Yes, without a shadow of doubt. In fact, it is said that at the onset of the battle he would tell his men, "Bear witness before the governor, that I was the first to launch an arrow against Husayn!" But even throughout the battle, there were some hesitations and reluctancies. Not to commit the overall crime of fighting Husayn or oppressing him, but to what extent would they go in the specific acts of injustice. How far would they go in chipping away at their humanity? Umar would tell his men to back away when Lady Zaynab sat at the body of her brother Husayn in his final moments. But soon after Husayn's death, he would have his men trample his beheaded body with the hooves of their horses.

Even Shimr, the eventual killer of Husayn, would heed to Husayn's request at one point to leave his women and children alone when they had decidedly moved to attack the tents. Husayn beseeched their customs as Arabs and told them to stay clear from his camp so long as he was alive. Shimr complied. Yet, it was Shimr who would take the task that no other soldier dared to take and beheaded Husayn, saying that he did so knowing that he was the grandson of Islam's Prophet. Indeed, it may have reflected the complexity of some of these characters, but it should not be misinterpreted for any excuse for the crimes they committed. Instead, it was this very toing and froing, this hypocrisy and inconsistency, that added to the gravity of Husayn's tragedy. The confusion, the duplicity, the falseness – the crime in the name of Islam – that is what made it so much worse. They spoke of God and killed His vicegerent. Husayn was not only the Prophet's grandson, he was the greatest semblance left of him on earth – and they all knew it. Husayn reminded them of the deed they were about to commit. Yet, with all the reminders they chose to take Husayn's life and his sacred blood would forever be on their hands.

The story of Imam Husayn is truly a saga of hope for every human being. Regardless of one's faith or creed, you cannot be but moved by Husayn's selfless sacrifice for God in the pursuit of saving his fellow man. For if Husayn's saga were to be described in but a few words, it would be that story of hope and the unrelenting door of salvation for every man and woman. He took his enemies on that day and gave them a chance for redemption, over and over again. Some took it and saved themselves, like the legendary Hur al-Riyahi, while most dug themselves deeper into their abyss of damnation. Husayn's every move was for a cause greater than himself and any man. Nothing about Husayn's story points the reader of his tragedy in any direction other than the Divine.

The remembrance of Husayn was catalyzed by his family members and close followers. After the tragedy of Ashura, they continued to call his name and beseech his light. They did not stop. They pledged never to forget his sacrifice and the blood that stained the sands of Karbala. They pledged to echo the name of Husayn across the valleys of eternity.

Husayn. Husayn. Husayn.

That name lives in the heart of every freedom-lover and seeker of light, whether they can make out the word or not. The name of Husayn echoes in the principles of humanity that reign true with every human being. He is that ship of salvation and light of guidance for every earnest seeker of truth. He is the path of God and the gateway to His eternal love.

Husayn did not merely fight for justice or stand up against oppression, though he did so ever so valiantly. Husayn did not

xviii | HUSAYN: THE SAGA OF HOPE

merely refuse to succumb to the immeasurable pressures of the political elite, though he did so with the greatest stride of confidence and trust in God. Husayn did not merely face off an army of thirty thousand without hesitation, though he did so with the greatest courage and bravery. Husayn should not be sung as merely another hero in history who fought for a cause and died for it. Instead, Husayn should be remembered as the savior of God's last and final message, the guardian of its pristine faith, the custodian of its truth. He was the leader who would sacrifice everything he had for people he would never see, and for generations not yet born.

Any person who comes to know the story of Husayn will be moved, inspired, and stirred for change. Husayn does not merely elicit an emotional response from the reader of his narrative that drives action. Instead, Husayn's life and death invoke and continue to bring to life an innate longing for truth and divine justice. When you read Husayn's story, you want to be with him. You wish that you would have had the honor to choose him, like his loyal companions did, against all the odds. You dream of the glory that came with serving the greatest cause and the greatest sacrifice that humanity had witnessed through the person of Husayn ibn Ali. You wish that you could have been there to protect him. You wish you could have sacrificed your own soul so that he could be spared. You wish to serve him, but you realize that you could do nothing to change his fate. That is because Husayn was God's chosen one. His sacrifice could not be replaced by anyone or anything else. It was the Prophet's beloved Husayn who was destined to save the religion. Surely, he met his destiny and did just that.

Husayn saw God's glory even in the most gruesome tragedy that he faced. His sacrifice was the will of God. It was the necessary catalyst for change and the spark for reformation for a nation on the verge of death. Husayn brought a nation back to life after its dreadful spiritual depression. He continues to bring that nation back to life. That is what is most beautiful about this story: it echoes throughout the centuries. The story will never die. That is because what he lived and died for what was greater than any man, any power, and any pursuit. Husayn lived and died for God. This was not a vague calling to fight in the way of God as various groups have misappropriated such a notion throughout history. Rather, Husayn lived and died for the sanctity of God's final and most complete message. Husayn sacrificed all that he had to save God's religion God promised that His word would be protected. Husayn protected it. He cemented and crystalized the religion of Islam to be preserved for hundreds and thousands of years to come.

> If the religion of my grandfather Muhammad is not to remain except by my death, then, O swords, take me.

The famous 19th century Arab poet, Shaykh Muhsin Abul-Hab, wrote these words from the perspective of Husayn's eternal stance on the plains of Karbala.

The land that will forever be remembered for his blood. What a heart and what a soul. What a man to go against all the odds without a shadow of doubt in his mind. His conviction was so clear that after each calamity he faced, after every son he lost in battle, that with each fallen comrade, he only looked up to the heavens and prayed:

Take from me my Lord, take so that You are pleased with me.

Like that, Husayn gave. He gave it all. God honored him. If a reader is looking for more than an inspiring story, but rather a life-changing experience of truth, of honor, of love – then the reader has come to the right place. The reader has come to Husayn: The Saga of Hope.

Before delving into the chapters of this book before you, I invite the reader to look at the brief excerpts I have included on the following pages. These excerpts come from the reflections of western scholars over the past few centuries, on what they took away from Husayn's story and the tragedy of Ashura. Their words served as a personal inspiration for me in seeing the tragedy of Husayn through the eyes of various readers.

Edward G. Brown (1862 – 1926), Sir Thomas Adams Professor of Arabic and Oriental Studies at the University of Cambridge:

> *...a reminder of the blood-stained field of Karbala, where the grandson of the Apostle of God fell at length, tortured by thirst and surrounded by the bodies of his murdered kinsmen, has been at anytime since then sufficient to evoke, even in the most lukewarm and heedless, the deepest emotions, the most frantic grief, and an exaltation of spirit before which pain, danger and death shrink to unconsidered trifles.*

– A Literary History of Persia (London, 1919).

Ignaz Goldziher (1850-1921), famous Hungarian orientalist and literary scholar:

Ever since the black day of Karbala, the history of this family... has been a continuous series of sufferings and persecutions. These are narrated in poetry and prose, in a richly cultivated literature of martyrologies - a Shi'i specialty - and form the theme of Shi'i gatherings in the first third of the month of Muharram, whose tenth day is kept as the anniversary of the tragedy at Karbala. Scenes of that tragedy are also presented on this day of commemoration in dramatic form. 'Our feast days are our assemblies of mourning.' So concludes a poem by a prince of Shi'i disposition recalling the many mihan [i.e. tribulations] of the Prophet's family. Weeping and lamentation over the evils and persecutions suffered by the 'Alid family, and mourning for its martyrs: these are things from which loyal supporters of the cause cannot cease. 'More touching than the tears of the Shi'is' has even become an Arabic proverb.

– Introduction to Islamic Theology and Law (Princeton, 1981).

Reynold Alleyne Nicholson (1868 – 1945), Sir Thomas Adams Professor of Arabic at the University of Cambridge:

Husayn fell, pierced by an arrow, and his brave followers were cut down beside him to the last man. Muhammadan tradition, which with rare exceptions is uniformly hostile to the Umayyad dynasty, regards Husayn as a martyr and Yazid as his murderer.

– A Literary History of the Arabs (Cambridge, 1930).

Peter J. Chelkowski (b. 1933), Professor of Middle Eastern Studies, New York University:

> *Husayn accepted and set out from Mecca with his family and an entourage of about seventy followers. But on the plain of Karbala, they were caught in an ambush set by the... caliph, Yazid. Though defeat was certain, Hussein refused to pay homage to him. Surrounded by a great enemy force, Hussein and his company existed without water for ten days in the burning desert of Karbala. Finally, Husayn, the adults and some male children of his family and his companions were cut to bits by the arrows and swords of Yazid's army; his women and remaining children were taken as captives to Yazid in Damascus. The renowned historian Abu Reyhan al-Biruni states; '... then fire was set to their camp and the bodies were trampled by the hoofs of the horses; nobody in the history of the humankind has seen such atrocities.*

– Ta'ziyeh: Ritual and Drama in Iran (New York, 1979)

Sir William Muir (1819-1905), Scottish scholar, statesman, and foreign secretary to India:

> *The tragedy of Karbala decided not only the fate of the caliphate, but of the Mohammedan kingdoms long after the Caliphate had waned and disappeared.* – Annals of the Early Caliphate (London, 1883).

CHAPTER 1

IN THE PROPHET'S ARMS

Husayn is of me and I am of him, God loves those who love Husayn.

– The Prophet Muhammad

Husayn's sacrifice in Karbala was destiny. The whole world would weep for his tragedy. Centuries would pass and the denizens of the Heaven and Earth could never forget Husayn and his triumphant tragedy. The angels of the Heavens cried a rain so vast, while the people of Earth swam in the rivers of their tears. They wailed, they cried, they mourned Husayn. But the first man to shed tears for his Husayn would do so before his tragedy had even begun.

The Holy Prophet Muhammad welcomed the news of his grandson with a smile so great and an embrace even greater. He came to the house of Fatima hastily, but within reach of the home, he slowed his steps. His feet grew heavy, like his aching heart. Asma opened the door for him with a smile, but soon turned to concern as she saw his distressed face.

"Dear Asma, bring me my child," the Prophet uttered in a choked voice.

Asma quickly grabbed the baby boy and brought him to his grandfather. Muhammad cradled his grandson in his arms and kissed him. The Prophet recited the *adhan* in his grandson's right ear and the *iqama* in his left. The call to prayer in his grandfather's voice was the first thing the newborn heard.

"Husayn," the Prophet smiled. "That is your name."

After a few moments, the Prophet was overcome by grief. He could not hold back his tears. He kissed him again and again, all the while weeping over this newborn baby.

Asma watched him nearby. Taken aback, she could not hold herself but ask, "What has grieved you, O Messenger of God, when your grandson has just entered your arms?"

The Prophet looked up from his grandson to Asma. The whites of his eyes had turned red and tears streamed down his cheeks.

"I weep for this son of mine," the Prophet replied.

"But he has just been born, my master!" Asma exclaimed.

"My son will be slain by a most audacious lot," the Prophet replied in grief.

Asma gasped. "Who will kill him?"

"An unjust group shall slay him after me," the Prophet said. "May the Almighty Allah deprive them of my intercession."

The Prophet stood up and handed the newborn boy to Asma. He whispered, "Do not share this news with Fatima just yet."

Two years later, the Prophet embarked on a journey to Iraq. His caravan crossed the desert plains as it had done so many times before. This time, however, was different. The Prophet ordered the caravan to stop abruptly. His steed neighed. The sun scorched above. Everything was still.

"To Allah we belong and to Him we shall return," the Prophet recited as his eyes filled with tears.

His company got off their horses and walked to their prophet in growing angst. Why have they stopped so suddenly and why was their prophet crying? They inquired most politely to the pained Prophet.

"Angel Gabriel is here," the Prophet took a deep breath. "He tells me of this place called Karbala."

The Prophet paused and the men waited.

"That is where my son, Husayn, will be slain mercilessly."

"Dear Prophet, who would dare slay your most beloved grandson?" one of the men asked in shock.

"A man named Yazid will have him killed," the Prophet replied. "May God have no mercy on him. He will order for my son's severed head and it will be presented to him."

They returned to Medina, where the Prophet immediately took to his pulpit and spoke to his people. They gathered around and sat before their prophet. He ascended and began in God's highest name. Beside the Prophet sat Ali with his two sons Hasan and Husayn in his arms.

"O' Allah, bear witness, I am your servant and messenger, Muhammad. I will leave my beloved sons to my nation. Your trusted Gabriel has revealed to me that this son of mine…" the

Prophet paused as he pointed at Husayn in Ali's arms, "will be deserted by my nation and slain ruthlessly."

The people in attendance gasped in disbelief.

"May Allah bless my son endlessly and make him the Chief of the Martyrs. You, my Lord, are the all-capable. You have power over everything. Do not have mercy over those who leave my son and kill him."

The people in the Prophet's Mosque burst into cries. They wailed and moaned the news of this prophetic tragedy. Upon their cries, the Prophet retorted:

"You are crying now. When the time comes, will you help him?" The cries grew louder. The Prophet turned his face to the Heavens. "O Allah, You are my son's guardian and protector."

The Prophet's face turned white as he looked on with worried eyes. He continued in his sermon to the people. Tears flowed from his eyes as he spoke.

"Know that I will leave with you two weighty things, the Book of God and my Progeny. The two shall not separate from each other till they arrive to me at the Pool of Kawthar in Paradise. All I ask is that you do right by my near of kin. Be mindful of this so that you meet me at that Pool having done right by my progeny…"

The people nodded as they wiped away the tears from their eyes. Some hearts were heavy, some indifferent. Some eyes shed tears, while others were dry as the desert.

The Holy Prophet went on to describe the scene of 'The Three Flags' on the Day of Judgment. The three flags represented three distinct groups of people that would come before the Holy Prophet on that day of reckoning. The first group would come before him holding a dark flag. The angels would look on with terror in their eyes, distraught by this group of men.

"Who are you?" the Prophet would ask this group.

"We are Arabs and followers of Monotheism," they would reply.

"And I am Muhammad, the Prophet of the Arabs and non-Arabs alike," he would respond.

"O Muhammad, we are from your followers," they would say as they knelt before him.

Muhammad would reply to them with a simple question: "How did you treat my Progeny and the Book of my Lord after me?"

"We wasted the Book and tore it to pieces. As for your Progeny, we followed them till they departed from the world."

The Prophet stated that he would turn away from this group in disgust and promised that such a group would remain thirsty on the Day. Another group would come forward, holding a dark flag as well, but this one was almost pitch black.

"Who are you?" the Prophet asked them.

"We are believers in God, and we are from your followers," the second group replied.

"And how did you behave with the weighty things I left behind – the Book of God and my Progeny?"

"We contradicted the Book of God and we abandoned your Progeny. And in all conditions, we considered them useless for us," was their candid response, as no truth could be veiled on that day.

"Leave me at once!" the Prophet would dismiss them.

After the two groups would leave the presence of the Prophet, a third flag would emerge. This flag was different. It radiated light. The group that surrounded this flag luminated with a beautiful aura.

"Who are you?" the Prophet would inquire.

"We are the followers of Monotheism. We are the servants of Muhammad and we are the survivors among the people of Truth. We have followed the Book of our Lord and considered its lawful as lawful and considered its unlawful as unlawful. We loved the Progeny of our Prophet Muhammad and we helped them like we helped ourselves. We supported them in battle and fought their opponents."

The Prophet would become jubilant and welcome them with open arms. "Congratulations! Congratulations!" he would say to his lot of true followers. "I am Muhammad, your Prophet." The group would be overjoyed by the Prophet's embrace. He would kneel down to the waters of the Pool of Paradise and pour them drinks by his own hand.

The Prophet ended his sermon exclaiming, "Indeed, Gabriel has informed me that my community shall slay my son, Husayn, on the land of Karbala. May God have no mercy upon the killers of Husayn until the Day of Reckoning."

It was clear to the *Muhajiroon* and the *Ansar*, those who migrated with the Prophet from Mecca and those who welcomed his arrival in Medina, that upon them was a fate of Husayn's blood. What role they would play in its unfolding could only be told in the years to come.

In the House of the Prophet, however, there was a consistency like no other. Wisdom was king, and the masters of it were Muhammad and Ali. In the arms of the Prophet, Husayn would grow, and in the shadow of his father, Ali, he would walk. Husayn moved as Ali moved. He went where he went. He spoke as he spoke. He ate as he ate. He breathed as he breathed. At a tender age, the Commander of the Faithful, Ali spoke to his son Husayn as he would speak to a man of age. He engaged his intellect and regarded him not as a boy, but as far greater. Throughout his childhood, Husayn was spoken to by his elders with such sophistication, it was no wonder that he would rise brilliantly. In a series of heartfelt directives, his father Ali advised his son:

My son, I advise you to fear Allah, the Mighty and the Sublime, in concealed and open matters and I make bequest to you to observe truth in happiness, thrift in wealth and poverty, justice with friend and enemy, work in happiness and sadness and satisfaction from the Almighty Allah in hard times and prosperity.

Son, no hardship is bad after which there is Paradise and no goodness is good after which there is Hell. Every bounty is less than Paradise and every calamity is lesser than the Fire of Hell. Know, my son, that one who is aware of his own faults, he does not find fault of others. And one who is satisfied with the fate of Almighty, he is not distraught with what he loses. And one who exposes others, his own defects shall be exposed. And one who ignores his own sins, he regards the sins of others as great. And one who puts himself into hardship of useless actions stumbles (suffers). And one that throws himself into the sea, drowns.

One who follows his own opinion becomes deviated. And one who considers himself needless of his own intellect, commits mistakes. And one who is arrogant to the people is degraded. One who behaves with them in foolish manner is abused. And one who sits in a bad place is put to blame. And one who cultivates the company of scholars gains honor. And one who jokes too much is not considered serious. And one who keeps aloof remains safe. One who leaves off the sensual desires gains independence. And one who leaves jealousy, gains the love of people.

My son, the respect of the believer is in his needlessness of the people. And contentment is unending wealth. One who remembers death too much remains content with little of the world and one who comes to know that his word is considered as his action, he becomes a man of few words, except where it is beneficial for him.... Remembrance is effulgence, carelessness is darkness, and ignorance is misguidance and fortunate is one who takes lesson from others. Manners are the best inheritance and good behavior is the best companion.

There is no bounty and progress for the one who cuts off relations. Salvation is made of ten parts. Nine parts of it are in silence but except that one remembers God and one of it is leaving off company of fools. One who decorates his gatherings with disobedience of God receives humiliation and one who seeks knowledge becomes intelligent.

My son, the beginning of knowledge is moderation, and its calamity is concealing it. And from the treasure of faith is patience in calamities. Chastity is the embellishment of poverty and thankfulness is the embellishment of wealth. One who does a thing too much is recognized by it. One who speaks too much makes too many mistakes and one who makes too many mistakes reduces his shame and one in whom shame is reduced, his abstemiousness reduces and one in whom abstemiousness reduces, his heart becomes dead and whoever's heart dies, he shall enter the Fire.

Do not make any sinner hopeless, because many a times it had been such that someone continued to sin, but his ultimate end was good. And many a times it had been that people performed many good deeds, but in their last days they destroyed them and are condemned to Hell-fire. One who gets the end of the matter, it becomes easy for him....

No status is higher than submission to God, no gift is higher than piety, and no refuge is more satisfactory than abstemiousness and no intercessor is better than repentance. No dress is more beautiful than salvation and no wealth is more effective in removing poverty than satisfaction while possessing power. One who makes efforts to get only as much as he needs, he has made haste in gaining his comfort and he has tried to maintain his reputation.

Greed is the key of sorrow, vehicle of hardship and cause of falling into sins. Evil deeds bring bad traits and defects. And for training of self, it is sufficient that one pays attention to that which one does not like for others and it is for your brother just as it is for your own self....

Thoughtfulness and consideration before initiating anything will keep you safe from regret. And one who carefully analyses the actions and studies them fully recognizes the points of mistakes. Patience is a shield against poverty. Opposition of the self creates perfection in oneself.

Hours eat away at age. Your Lord is the best of the rulers for the oppressors and He is cognizant of what is hidden. The worst provision for the Day of Judgment is oppression on people... No bounty shall he receive except after separating from another bounty. How near is comfort to exhaustion, and poverty to bounty, and death to life, thus blessed is the one who has made special for Allah, the knowledge and action, love and hatred, taking and leaving, speaking and keeping quiet.

And congratulations to the scholar who is aware and refrains from sins and acts and makes efforts and is fearful of destruction and loss. Thus, he is prepared and ready. If he is asked, he replies clearly, and if he is released, he remains silent. His speech should be correct, and his silence should be due to the inability to reply. Woe, and all woe on the one who is disappointed, degraded and sinful. And what he does not like for others, he considers it good for himself. One who has softness in his speech, his love becomes incumbent. One who does not have shame and generosity, his death is better than his life. Generosity of a person is not perfected till it is not important for him which of his two dresses he should wear and which of his two foods he should eat.

My son, honor Allah in all that you do…

As a young boy, Husayn was immersed in this tradition of wisdom and piety. From his grandfather to his father and mother, Husayn swam in the seas of knowledge. He was far beyond his years. Thus, he could withstand what other children could not. And as an adult, he would endure and sacrifice what no other man could. From his childhood, Husayn was reminded of his tragic fate and ultimate sacrifice.

One day, Husayn and his older brother Hasan were playing with their grandfather, Muhammad. After some play, the Prophet playfully grabbed them both and sat the young boys on his lap. He embraced them both with his beautiful radiant smile. They looked up at him and smiled back. There was nothing quite like his warmth and love. The Prophet hugged and kissed Hasan on the mouth. He then hugged and kissed Husayn on the neck. After some moments of play, Husayn got up and walked into the next room where his mother Fatima was preparing some lentils. Fatima looked up and smiled at her son, who she found to be occupied in thought.

"What is on your mind dear?" she asked Husayn.

"Well, my grandfather kissed my brother Hasan on the mouth but kissed me on my neck. I am wondering, why did he not kiss me on the mouth like Hasan?"

Fatima smiled, "My dear, let us wait together for your grandfather and then we will ask him." Reassured, Husayn stayed with his mother and helped her prepare the lentils.

Later in the day, Ali had come home and they all came to sit together in the living area. Sitting altogether, Fatima brought up Husayn's question to her father, Muhammad. Hasan and Husayn were sitting beside their mother Fatima, while Ali sat next to the Prophet. The Prophet went into prostration for a moment and then raised his head.

My dear Fatima, it is heavy on my heart to relay this to you, but I must. Hasan will be poisoned to death, thus I kissed him on the place that will cause his martyrdom.

And I kissed Husayn on his neck because he will be slaughtered. I kissed him on the place of where the swords will strike and sever his holy neck.

Fatima's face became pasty white. Her chest tightened. Her mouth became dry. "Father, my Husayn is going to be killed and slaughtered?" she managed to ask in disbelief.

"Yes, my dear," the Prophet said with heaviness in his voice. "And in a time where none of us will be alive. Husayn will be without us."

"He will be martyred in a time without us! Dear father, then who will be with him? Who will commemorate him? Who will cry over him?" Fatima cried.

The Prophet got up and consoled Fatima. "My dear Fatima, this is his fate. But know that God will give Husayn true lovers and loyal followers that will come to commemorate him. They will strike their chests in sorrow and cry over his tragedy until the Day of Reckoning."

As Fatima wiped away her tears and embraced her son Husayn she said, "How shall we reward these honorable people?"

"I will be their intercessor on the Day of Judgment," the Prophet replied.

"And I will lead them myself into Heaven by the hand," Fatima promised.

The Prophet turned to Ali and asked him, "What about you O' Ali? What will you do for these loyal followers who will commemorate your son?"

"I will quench their thirst by my hand at the Fountain of Paradise," Ali replied with a sorrowful voice.

"And I shall walk them along the path into Heaven!" the young Hasan contributed as he looked at his grandfather and then back at Husayn. Husayn was now sitting with his head down between his knees. A moment of silence passed. They all looked to Husayn.

"What about you Husayn?"

"Me?" the young Husayn replied. "They should know that whoever remembers me and visits me, I will remember them and visit them. I will never leave them. I will be with them in the hour of death, when the soul is taken from the body, and in the grave."

I will never leave them.

When time had come for Husayn's grandfather to depart this world, it was especially difficult for the young Husayn. He was only six years old. In his last moments, the Prophet felt the pangs of death. When Husayn saw his grandfather moaning, he rushed to him and threw his arms around him.

"Grandfather, I am here."

"My beloved Husayn," the Prophet whispered. He hugged him tight and it was as if the pain had all gone away. But the agony of his soul's departing would soon be replaced with the painful thought of Husayn's death. For with every joy that the Prophet felt from Husayn's smile, he would be reminded of Husayn's future fate in Karbala.

"What have we done to Yazid?!" the Prophet cried. "Dear God, do not have mercy on my son's killer!"

The Prophet went unconscious with Husayn still on his chest. When he woke up, he found Husayn laying on him with his arms on his sides. The Prophet embraced his grandson once more and would not let go.

"My dear Husayn," the Prophet repeated as tears fell from his eyes and on to his cold cheeks.

"Though I will not be there with you on your day, know that I will face your oppressors before God on the Day of Reckoning."

CHAPTER 2

AFTER THE MESSENGER

There is no one more truthful under the sky from amongst my companions than Abuthar.

– The Prophet Muhammad

Husayn grew up as a young man in his grandfather's footsteps. When people missed the presence of God's Messenger, they looked for Husayn. He walked like him. He talked like him. He smelled like him. He felt like him. People could feel the warmth of their late prophet through Husayn. And as people beseeched their prophet for help, they too would go to Husayn to ask their needs.

One day, as Husayn was busy working outside of his home, a Bedouin came to him. Dressed in simple clothing and a turban wrapped loosely around his head, he saluted the Prophet's grandson.

"Asalaamu Alaykum Master Husayn," he said.

"Wa Alaykum Asalaam." Husayn replied with a smile.

"I had the honor of enjoying the presence of your grandfather while he was still alive," the Bedouin said. "I heard him say,

'Whenever you have any need, ask it from one of four kinds of people.'"

"And who would those be?"

"A noble Arab, a generous person who gives happily, the people of the Quran, and those with illuminating faces."

"I see."

"And I only see those features manifested in you, sir."

"And how is that?"

"The Arabs are noble only because of your grandfather. As for generosity and benevolence, you are the master. The Quran was revealed in your house, so you are its people. Finally, I heard the Holy Prophet say, 'When you desire to see me, just look at the faces Hasan and Husayn.'"

Husayn nodded slowly and smiled.

"You see I could only ask my need from you…"

"And what is your request?" Husayn asked.

The Bedouin proceeded to write his request in the sand with a small stick. Husayn watched him.

"My father Ali says that goodness is proportionate to divine recognition," Husayn stated. "So I want to ask you a few questions. If you answer one, I shall give you one third of what I have. If you answer two, then I will give you two thirds of what I possess. And if you answer all of the questions, all I have in my possession will be yours."

"Go on and ask the questions," the Bedouin replied anxiously. "There is no power and strength save in God." The Bedouin prayed. Husayn asked his first question.

"What is the best deed?"

"Belief in God," the Bedouin replied.

"What is the way of salvation for man?" Husayn followed.

"To rely on and trust in God."

"What is it that bestows beauty to man?"

"Knowledge accompanied with forbearance."

"What if he does not have these?"

"Then he should have wealth accompanied with generosity."

"What if he does not have these?"

"Then he should have poverty accompanied with patience."

"What if he does not have these either?"

"A bolt of lightning should strike him from the sky and burn him up."

Husayn smiled and handed the Bedouin a purse filled with all the money in his possession. His generosity was no accident. Friends and foes alike admired the young Husayn. One could not but love the young man who looked so much like the Prophet of God. But no matter how much he looked like the Messenger, Husayn was eighteen years old when Uthman was chosen by Umar's council to rule the Muslim empire as its third caliph. First as a boy and now as a young man, he watched the administrations of the first caliphates rise and plunder their way through dominance. Husayn quietly observed his father as he continuously provided advice to the caliphate. He noted his father's close proximity to decision-making. He knew that his father was not fond of these men, nor did he approve of their positions. He knew that they had taken that which was not theirs. So, Husayn watched.

Husayn watched and learned as his father Ali navigated a new system that was built to replace him. Though that system usurped his own rights, Husayn's father would swallow the jagged blade for the sake of the faith that his family would live and die for. Husayn watched his father as he endured the agony of advising in the courts of the first and second caliphates, all for the purpose of safeguarding the institution of faith and the rights of its people. The reign of Uthman, however, was especially heinous.

The crimes committed by Uthman's administration against the companions of the Holy Prophet were intolerable. Still, Husayn, his father, and brother had no choice but to endure and choose patience throughout the adversities they witnessed. Even until the very end of Uthman's caliphate, when the rebels had gathered around the caliph's house wanting to burn it to the ground, Ali and his sons would stand for unity and brotherhood. Ali had even instructed Hasan and Husayn to dress in their battle-gear to defend the house of Uthman against the havoc that the rebels wished to ensue. Nevertheless, the pain and anguish the caliphate had caused the people was too much to bear.

Uthman's extravagance, nepotism, and disregard for the people would bring about his end. The built-up anger and frustration with the caliphate was not a surprise after the institutionalized disparities and injustice experienced by the people. Even some of the closest companions of the Prophet were openly tortured, exiled, and killed under the orders of Uthman's administration. Husayn and his family patiently endured while trying to preserve what was left of their grandfather's nation. Perhaps the story of Abuthar is the best example of Husayn's experience during the twelve-year reign of the third caliphate.

Abuthar was one of the foremost companions of Husayn's grandfather, the Prophet Muhammad. Abuthar was known for his piety, knowledge, and love for peace and justice. The Prophet loved Abuthar and trusted him with secrets he would not entrust to others. He promised him Paradise and assured him of his reward with God. Abuthar carried on with that promise. His heart was warm with the Prophet's words. Abuthar was very protective of the religion and was known to stand up for it wherever he could; thus, the reign of Uthman proved to be extremely difficult for him.

Abuthar was critical of Uthman's administration. He was particularly vocal about the economic policies of his leadership that were blatantly corrupt and disenfranchised those who were not in the caliph's circle of nepotism. Abuthar brought such criticisms directly to Uthman in his open court.

"You cannot be doing this, your policies are disuniting people and ruining their lives," Abuthar would proclaim.

Uthman did not heed his words and turned away instead. As the treasury continued to recite grants for the chiefs of Uthman's clan and the Umayyad tribe, Abuthar stood up and recited a verse from the Holy Quran with the loudest of his voice:

"... And as for those who hoard up gold and silver and do not spend it in Allah's way, announce to them a painful chastisement." (Holy Quran 9:34)

One of the recipients of Uthman's grants was Marwan ibn Al-Hakam, who was particularly angered by Abuthar's vocal objection. Marwan was a relative of Uthman's whom the caliph brought out of exile and into a government post within his administration. Marwan and his father were exiled by the Prophet over a decade earlier.

When Abuthar left the session, Marwan stayed afterwards to discuss the matter with his cousin, Uthman.

"That man has become a nuisance," Marwan said irritably.

"That I agree with," Uthman replied.

"I would assume that you will take care of this nuisance, as the family should not need to put up with such people."

Uthman nodded and reassured him it would be taken care of. When Abuthar returned to the next session in Uthman's court, Uthman summoned him again.

"You are to refrain from further objections in my court, Abuthar," Uthman commanded.

"What objections do you speak of?"

"The matter you recited earlier."

"The verse of God I recited earlier?"

"Yes."

"Does Uthman prohibit me from reciting the Book of God?"

Uthman did not reply. The spectators present watched closely. The hall was silent They could hear a pin drop.

"By Allah, I cannot offend Allah for the sake of Uthman. The displeasure of Uthman is better for me than the displeasure of Allah," Abuthar stated firmly then walked out of the session.

Uthman was humiliated, as all eyes were on him as he was told off by the humble old Abuthar. The caliph contained himself and prepared for Abuthar's next outcry. He would not let this go so easily.

Days later, Abuthar found himself in the assembly once again. He attended to correct wrongs and voice objections to any misgivings that threatened the sanctity of the religion. He was a zealous advocate of the preservation of Islam. In this particular session, Uthman asked those present a legal question pertaining to state funds.

"Is it allowed for one to borrow some money from the public treasury and when it is possible to return it?"

One of Uthman's friends and confidants, Kaab al-Ahbar, quickly replied with a verdict. "Yes, such a transaction is permissible. You are in the right to do so, sir."

Uthman nodded agreeably, delighted with such quick verification by his most trusted and objective group of advisors. Abuthar, however, looked around at the assembly, simply dumbfounded.

"Will no one say anything about this audacity?" Abuthar cried out. "Since when do we take the laws of our faith from a Jew?!" Abuthar shouted, pointing at Ka'b.

Uthman grew infuriated. He stood from his throne and yelled down at Abuthar, eyes bulging, red in the face.

"You continue to be a pain in my side and now you insult my friends! I have had enough of you," Uthman looked to the guards at his side. "Have him removed from my court. You are banished to Syria, Abuthar!"

Within hours, Abuthar was kicked out of Medina and sent away to Syria. Uthman thought that with Abuthar far away from Medina, Abuthar could cause him no trouble. Little did he know that Abuthar's voice would travel the mountains of Syria and the deserts of Arabia.

Though Abuthar was no longer privy to the activities of Caliph Uthman, now he found an opportunity to observe the functions of Uthman's governor in Syria – Muawiya ibn Abu Sufyan. When Abuthar arrived in Damascus, it was not long before he attended the assembly of the governor and witnessed the way it conducted business in Syria.

Muawiya was worse than Uthman. He operated in such a liberal fashion with the funds of the public treasury, with no oversight or checks to his programs. Ordinary people were taxed on

their hard work, funding the treasury of the state that would pro-
duce projects for the common good. Abuthar attended the sessions of the treasury and found little good to be common.

In one of the sessions of the treasury, which Muawiya pre-
sided over, the budget for the governor's new palace was being
proposed. Abuthar was shocked to hear the details of the new
construction and the extravagance it brought forth, all to be
funded by the people's tax contributions. Before the budget was
formally approved, Abuthar raised his voice in protest.

"I must voice my deep concern," Abuthar began. "If this palace is being financed from public funds, it is surely breaching the
trust of its people."

Some of the meeting's members gasped. Others gawked at
Abuthar's alleged insolence. Muawiya's brows tensed as he
stared Abuthar down.

Abuthar continued, "And if such a palace is being financed
by your own personal funds, Muawiya, then it is surely an extravagance unbecoming of a leader in Muhammad's nation."

"Who are you to question us?" Muawiya shouted.

"I am a Muslim of this nation, concerned for its health and
wealth," Abuthar replied.

"The wealth is the wealth of God! And we are its guardians to
use as we see fit," Muawiya snapped at Abuthar.

"The wealth is the wealth of the people, and you are accountable to them before God," Abuthar replied wittily, and left the
session of the treasury.

Muawiya turned to one of his officers and whispered, "Keep an eye on him."

"Yes sir," replied the officer, excusing himself from the session.

People followed him, admirers and foes alike, amazed by his confident demeanor and courage to speak. They saw in him not merely a man in protest, but a scholar in his own right, clarifying right from wrong in such a sensible manner. The more people followed him, the more Abuthar spoke. He did not hesitate to criticize the authorities and the state of the caliphate. He encouraged others to do the same.

"Those who rule over you are accountable to you," Abuthar told them. "That is your right upon them. They wish to tell you otherwise, but by God, such innovations that have gained currency these days as are not found in the Book of God or His Prophet's tradition. By Allah, I see that the truth is being effaced and falsehood is growing stronger. Truthful people are being falsified and sinners are being given preference over the virtuous."

As Abuthar's audiences grew, the authorities became increasingly anxious of Abuthar's presence in Syria. Though his goal was merely to educate and bring basic reform through spreading awareness, he was seen as a security threat to Muawiya's administration. Fearing unrest, Muawiya had an issue ordered prohibiting Abuthar from speaking publicly and forbidding others to congregate around him. If anyone was found to be in Abuthar's company, they would be punished by the fullest extent of state law.

Muawiya summoned Abuthar to his court to reprimand him for his political activities. Abuthar walked in dressed in his simple garb and turban. Muawiya sat upon his throne, dressed liked the princes of the Byzantine, looking down upon Abuthar.

"Why did you come to Syria?" Muawiya asked him.

"I came by the order of the Caliph Uthman," Abuthar replied simply.

"Yes, but what are you trying to do here, Abuthar?"

"Here? I am here by your order sir," Abuthar smiled.

"Enough!" Muawiya shouted. "You incite people against us and do what you do, O enemy of Allah! If I wished to kill a companion of Muhammad without the permission of the caliph, I would have killed you already!"

Abuthar's demeanor changed. He responded coldly, "I am not the enemy of God and neither an enemy of His Messenger. Rather, it is you and your father who are the enemies of God and Muhammad. You accepted Islam by your tongues but remain disbelievers in your hearts!" Abuthar turned around and walked out.

Muawiya was infuriated by Abuthar's boldness. He nodded with rage and whispered to himself, "I will be rid of you soon, you fool." Muawiya wrote to Uthman to have Abuthar returned back to Medina for him to deal with him personally. Uthman consented and instructed him as follows:

"Send him back on the bare back of a wild camel with an unruly driver. I will deal with him."

Abuthar was quickly summoned for his return to Medina and the terrible journey began. They did not let him rest his eyes and barely quenched his thirst with stingy portions of water. Blisters covered his feet and legs. The drivers accompanying him were specifically instructed to give him an excruciating time.

When they reached Medina, they took Abuthar directly to the court of Uthman. Abuthar arrived in an especially devastated state. He had thinned on the journey, his eyes were sunken and tired, and he could barely stand due to dehydration and fatigue. Uthman, however, did not hesitate to revile Abuthar.

"I sent you to Syria to be rid of your headaches and misbehavior, but you managed to make things even worse for yourself. You continue to spread this nonsense and act unruly as you are," Uthman said.

Abuthar took a deep breath, "I did nothing except that I gave you a piece of advice and you took it the wrong way. Thus, you sent me away to Syria where I advised Muawiya similarly. He also did not like it and he turned me out."

Uthman replied, "You are a liar! You are nursing sedition in your mind. You want to provoke the people against me!"

"O Uthman, if you at the very least followed Abu Bakr and Umar, nobody would say anything against you," Abuthar sighed.

Enraged, Uthman stood up and screamed, "What does it matter if I follow them or not? May your mother die!"

"By Allah, you cannot accuse me of anything except that I direct people to do good and prevent them from doing unlawful acts."

Filled with rage, Uthman turned to his courtiers and exclaimed, "Advise me as to what I should do with this old liar! Should I punish him with flogging, send him to the prison, execute him or exile him?"

Ali ibn Abi Talib walked into the session.

Hearing Uthman's bellowing, he interjected and said, "O Uthman, when our Holy Prophet Muhammad was alive, I heard him say: 'There is no speaker, under the sky and upon the Earth, more truthful than Abuthar.'"

Uthman sat back down and muttered, "Surely, he has created dissension in the Muslim community." Abuthar was so weak, he almost fell to the ground. Uthman dismissed him and carried on the business of the day.

Nevertheless, Abuthar did not heed to Uthman's threats or show of prowess. Instead, he continued his eloquent protest against the caliphate's politics and economic policies that were disenfranchising the people. His speech was as sharp as an Arabian sword.

"You collect children to recruit them as soldiers. You employ nepotism as a state policy, and you make the children of emancipated slaves proximate towards you," Abuthar calmly told off Uthman in his court.

"I hereby make it unlawful for anyone to be in the company of Abuthar!" Uthman proclaimed. But Abuthar did not stop. He spoke to the birds, he spoke to the wind, he spoke to anything with a soul. It did not matter if he was alone. His pursuit for justice and reformation was unwavering.

Uthman was fed up with Abuthar. He could not stand him any longer. Thus, he decided to have him exiled, banished from the lands of the inhabited. The caliph's royal guard arrested Abuthar and presented him before him in his court.

"You again?" Uthman said with scorn.

Abuthar replied, "Woe be to you, Uthman! Have you not seen the Holy Prophet? Have you not seen Abu Bakr and Umar? Did they behave in such a manner that you would deal with me like an oppressor?"

"I am done with you, old man! You are to leave us and never come back here again!" Uthman yelled out.

"Are you banishing me from the sanctuary of the Messenger of Allah?" Abuthar said softly.

"Yes, and it is because you have become a disgrace to this land," Uthman replied.

"Shall I leave for Mecca?" Abuthar asked.

"No."

"To Basra then?" Abuthar followed.

"No," Uthman said looking away.

"Where should I go?"

"You are exiled to Rabadha, and you will die there."

Uthman gave the exile orders to Marwan ibn Al-Hakam. He was explicitly ordered that no one was to see Abuthar before he left. No farewells, no goodbyes. He was to be disgraced and given no regard.

But the Prophet's family could not bear to leave Abuthar without a farewell, without words of reassurance, without telling him that all his work would not go in vain. And so, Abdullah ibn Jafar, Aqeel, Ammar, Ali, Hasan and Husayn would find Abuthar before his departure and give him a final embrace.

As they neared Abuthar, who was guarded by Marwan and his men, Marwan turned to Hasan ibn Ali and said sternly, "Beware, Hasan! Don't you know that Uthman has ordered not to speak to this man? If you didn't know it, know it now."

Ali walked in a few steps closer to Marwan, who sat upon his horse, and said, "Leave us and be away to the fire of Hell that awaits you!" Ali then slapped the steed and it went off running.

Humiliated, Marwan ran off to Uthman and told him that Ali ibn Abi Talib and his lot explicitly disobeyed the command of the caliphate and were in Abuthar's company as they spoke.

Ali took Abuthar in his arms and hugged him tight as tears fell from his eyes. He endured seeing his friend treated so harshly and now could not bear to see him leave. He gave a monologue of Abuthar's character and personality as he embraced his long-time friend and companion:

O Abuthar, you became angry for the sake of the Almighty. So, repose hope in the One for whom you became angry. Those people dread for their life from you and feared for your religion. Thus, you leave free in their hands that for which they feared you or that for which you feared them. Leave it! As how needy they are for that which you prevented them from and how needless you are from that which they prevented you from. And it shall be known tomorrow who has won and who shall be more vied. That if the Heavens and the Earth are closed for a servant and he had been pious, the Almighty Allah makes a way out for him. Nothing can give you consolation except the truth. The truth will be your companion in loneliness, and you can get alarmed only by falsehood. Because if you had accepted their world they would have loved you, and if you had torn with your teeth a thing from them, they would have given security to you."

Hasan shared some heartfelt words, as did the other companions amongst the group. Husayn then came forward to share his own grief and affection with Abuthar:

Dear uncle, you need not worry, as Allah has power over everything.... These people have kept their world from you, and you kept your religion away from them. And how needless were you of that which they denied you and how needful were they of that which you denied them. Thus, beseech the Almighty for patience and seek His refuge from impatience and greed, as patience is from religion and nobility and greed do not hasten sustenance and impatience does not delay death.

After all those words, Abuthar burst into tears, and he glanced for the last time at them and bid farewell to what he considered to be his own family – the Prophet's family. He then shared the words that emanated from his own heart, as he smiled through his falling tears:

> *When I saw you, I remembered the Holy Prophet and I immediately felt blessed. My beloved friends, you alone were the means of solace to me in Medina. Whenever I saw you, my heart was at ease and my mind was at peace. But now here we are... Just as I was a burden to Uthman in Hijaz, I was a burden to Muawiya in Syria. Uthman did not want to send me to Egypt because I would be a burden to his foster brother who is his governor there. Nor did he want to send me to a Basra, where his cousin rules and he feared I would be a thorn to his side. So, now, I am exiled to this desert where I do not have any supporter other than Allah. He is sufficient for me, He alone.*

Abuthar smiled and embraced his friends once more for the last time. And then he was off. Exiled to wander the desert, Abuthar would starve to death days later. People described Abuthar as having the mannerisms and humility of Jesus Christ. They likened him to the Ahlulbayt and the saints of Abraham's lineage. He lived and died for his cause, and his cause was truth. Husayn admired Abuthar and loved him. He was pained by his tragedy. He carried the memory of Abuthar in his heart like his father Ali, who promised to honor him.

When Ali returned to the city, after bidding farewell to Abuthar, a group of men hastily came to him to deliver the news.

"Uthman is enraged that you disobeyed his orders," one of the men said to Ali.

"Is that so?" Ali responded calmly.

"He requests your presence, sir," the man replied.

Ali walked into Uthman's court with his sons Hasan and Husayn by his side. When they came before Uthman, the caliph rose from his seat and sternly said to Ali, "Why did you disobey my commands?!"

"I did no such thing," Ali replied.

"You assaulted Marwan's horse when he tried to stop you," Uthman snapped back.

"Yes, Marwan came to me to prevent us, and I drove him away. But I did not disobey your command."

"Did you not know that I strictly forbade the people from bidding farewell to Abuthar?"

"Is it incumbent for us to obey your orders even if they conflict with the obedience of Allah and the truth?" Ali retorted.

"Pay up the penalty to Marwan."

"For what?" Ali asked.

"For slapping the ears of his mount."

"My horse is over there. If he wants, he can slap its ears like I did to his mount," Ali stated. "But, by Allah, if he abuses me, I shall abuse you in the same way. But what I say will be nothing but the truth."

"Why should he not abuse you if you have abused him? By Allah, you are not superior to him in my view."

Ali was shocked. The Holy Prophet exiled Marwan and his father during his own lifetime due to their mischief and enmity to the Muslims. Their exile ended by Uthman's order when he came to rule. Marwan was further awarded with a government post.

Ali stood up and looked Uthman square in the eye.

"Do you say this to me? You dare compare me to Marwan? I am, by Allah, superior to you and my father is better than your father and my mother is better than yours," Ali turned to the Heavens. "God you are the witness; these are the calamities I am bearing with these people."

Uthman fell silent and failed to give any response. Ali and his sons, Hasan and Husayn, walked out of the caliph's court.

CHAPTER 3

HIS FATHER'S CALIPHATE

By God, this shoe is more valuable than the caliphate they fight over. I only assume its position to establish truth and eradicate falsehood.

– Ali ibn Abi Talib

Uthman's twelve-year rule would finally come to end. The disenfranchised groups in the nation had enough of the corruption and nepotism. The people revolted. Civil unrest could no longer be contained. Uthman was killed. Husayn and his family had no role to play in this. In fact, they came to Uthman's aid against the rebels that wished to take his life. The rebels had surrounded Uthman's home and cut him off from food and water in his final days. Hasan and Husayn came to fend them off and even deliver water to the famished Uthman.

But the rebels would not stand down and threatened to kill anyone that stood in their way. Uthman's home would be overwhelmed. They would break in by the dozens through the windows and rooftops. Uthman would be apprehended by the rebels and killed in his home. The nation was in disarray. The people were distraught. How could this happen? They needed someone to rally around, someone who could lift them up and pick up the broken pieces, someone to save them from the abyss they were in. That someone was Husayn's father – Ali.

The nation begged Ali to ascend to the caliphate, though for Ali, it was no ascension at all.

"Go and seek someone else… I am better for you as counsel rather than chief," Husayn observed his father telling the people. "You will not have the patience for the justice of my rule," Ali asserted. But the people would not quit. They were adamant to have Ali rule after the death of Uthman. Ali finally acquiesced to the will of the people after warning them of what was to come. With his ascent, and the resulting four-and-a-half-year reign, came three civil wars – all of which occurred because others wished to oust Ali from the caliphate and claim it for themselves.

Husayn was thirty years old when his father took on the caliphate. During his father's short rule, Husayn would get married and have his first son, Ali, whom he named after his beloved father. What would naturally be a time of celebration, with getting married and starting a family, was instead plagued with three civil wars – Jamal, Siffin, and Nahrawan. Husayn and his older brother Hasan played strategic roles in each of these wars.

As Husayn, his brother and father prepared for one of the battles ahead, Abdullah ibn Abbas came before Imam Ali. He found Ali busy fixing the straps to a torn shoe of his.

"Peace be upon you, Commander of the Faithful," Abdullah said gracefully as he placed his hand on his chest.

"And peace be upon you," Ali replied. Before Abdullah could speak of the business he came forward with, Ali asked him, "What say you of the value of this shoe?"

Abdullah took a moment to examine the old shoe. As Ali continued to tug and pull at the raggedy thing, Abdullah discerned, "It does not seem to have any value at all."

Ali nodded. Abdullah waited as Ali continued to work at the torn shoe.

When Ali finally looked up after finishing his work, he said to Abdullah, "By God, this shoe is more valuable than the caliphate they fight over. I only assume its position to establish truth and eradicate falsehood."

Ali strapped his feet with the shoes he repaired and went into battle and risked his own life, time and time again, to save the lives of others. It was this sophisticated simplicity of justice and valor, wisdom and honor, that Husayn was raised with.

Husayn watched his father take on the challenges of his day without fear or hesitation, because his cause was so clear to him – to honor God and protect his fellow man. Ali would raise his sons to live their lives on the path of justice and truth, through the unfailing Quranic wisdom that, "What is to come is greater than what is now." (Quran 87:17).

For four and a half years, Husayn was with his father fighting injustices and fending off discord and disunity. He watched his father establish a standard of just governance that enfranchised the young, women, and minorities across the nation. Everyone was to be treated with honor and respect – friend and foe alike.

It is said that at the Battle of Nahrawan, the last of the three major civil wars during Imam Ali's caliphate, that Husayn was present in his father's army. The battle ended with Ali's clear victory over the Khawarij, a group that had defected from Ali's army at the end of the previous battle at Siffin. The Khawarij left Ali and sought to fight him because they decreed he was in error by not pursuing Muawiya and instead allowing for the *Tahkeem*, or arbitration, to take place. The Khawarij were a fanatic bunch who persecuted and killed anyone who did not share their beliefs, regardless of who they were.

When Ali's army claimed victory and the soldiers of the Khawarij were apprehended at the conclusion of the battle, an interesting thing happened that connects to Husayn and his fate decades later. It is said that while the Khawarij were apprehended, their wrists were tied with rope. Husayn ibn Ali was walking through the ranks of the defeated soldiers while one of them called out to him.

"Husayn! Husayn!"

Husayn stopped and turned around.

"They say that if you are asked, you never deny. I believe this to be true."

Husayn nodded. "What is your request?"

"Your father Ali ordered his men to tie these ropes way too tight. The fibers are digging into my skin and I am in pain. Could you loosen these ropes, Husayn?"

Husayn told him to wait for a moment. He went back to his father Ali and told him what had happened. Though he knew his father would never unjustly hurt another, even an enemy, Husayn asked him if he did not mind him loosening the ropes, since he was asked. Ali smiled and told his son to do whatever he saw fit.

Husayn returned to the soldier and loosened the ropes.

"Thank you, Husayn!" the soldier cried out. It is said that the soldier's name was Shimr ibn Thil-Jawshan.

The days continued as Ali and his sons faced off with the continued troubles brought forth by the power-hungry men who would not rest until they had what they sought. Muawiya was the chief adversary. He did everything he could to wreak havoc during Ali's caliphate. He would not rest until he was at the helm himself and rid of Ali.

In the holy month of Ramadan, Muawiya would do the unspeakable. He hired an assassin to kill Ali. The assassin's name was Abdulrahman ibn Muljam. Abdulrahman managed to strike Ali on the head as the caliph was prostrated in prayer in the Mosque of Kufa. That was perhaps the only way anyone could dare take the life of Ali ibn Abi Talib. Ali did not die instantly; instead, he painfully survived two more days as he suffered from the poison that laced Abdulrahman's sword.

It is said that Husayn was not in Kufa when his father was attacked. Husayn was stationed at the Nakhila encampment commanding a battalion from his father's army, getting ready to face off with Muawiya's troops once again. When the attempt on his father's life took place on the nineteenth of the month of Ramadan, Hasan immediately sent word to Husayn of what had transpired.

The messenger would ride like the wind. When he reached Husayn, the Imam was training some of the soldiers at the campground. The messenger jumped off his horse and knelt before the Imam.

"Master Husayn, my apologies, sir," the messenger said.

"What news do you bring from Kufa?"

The messenger handed a letter. "It is your father, the Commander of the Faithful, sir."

Husayn read the letter, then looked up at the messenger in disbelief. He mounted his horse and went straight to Kufa. The deepest sorrow overcame Husayn as he entered Kufa and found his father on his deathbed. When he saw his father, Husayn ran to his bedside and wrapped his arms around him. Ali was elated to see his beloved Husayn. Ali spoke to Husayn from the heart. The following were some of the final words Husayn heard from his father Ali:

> *My dear son! I want you to know… You are a part of my body and my soul. Whenever I look at you, I feel as if I am looking at myself. If any calamities befall you, I feel as if they have befallen me. Your death will make me feel as if it was my own death. Your affairs are to me like my own affairs.*

Ali ibn Abi Talib passed away on the twenty-first day of the holy month of Ramadan. Hasan and Husayn buried their father. They mourned the greatest man to walk God's earth after their grandfather Muhammad. Though Imam Ali's life was taken, his principles would live on through his sons. The next day's challenges were great, but so was their vision and forbearance.

CHAPTER 4

MUAWIYA'S DYNASTY

We are the Family of Prophethood. Our home is the place of God's angels and the House of Revelation. God started his creation with us, and He will end it with us.

– Husayn ibn Ali

With the peace accord struck between Husayn's brother, Hasan, and Muawiya, the latter would go on to rule for an unprecedented eighteen-year reign. Muawiya established the Umayyad caliphate and swore to expand the reach of his new empire and quell any dissent within it. It was eight years that Hasan lived under Muawiya's rule, before he was poisoned and killed. Husayn would survive his brother and now take on the active role of Imamate for his faithful followers. He would live under Muawiya's reign for ten long years after Hasan was killed.

Many of the Muslims of the empire did not see Muawiya for the corrupt leader that he was. They were taken by the glitter and glamor of his gold. Under Muawiya, the empire grew in wealth and material prosperity. Economically and militarily, it thrived. Spiritually, however, it was just about to shrivel and die. As the money poured in, people paid more attention to their coins and less to how they acquired it.

Eventually, Muawiya would grow ill and weak. To conceal his illness, the frail caliph ordered his servants to dress him in makeup, comb his hair with scented oils, and wrap his back to help him stand straight. He welcomed visitors to salute at a distance and see that he was alive and well. As the visitors came in one after the other, Muawiya grinned. *I am still here.* He reassured himself. He then recited a few words of poetry, praising his ingenuity:

Despite sickness and despite the hate of men

I shall show those who ridicule the son of Sufyan

That I stand against the hardship of time and season

As he recited, one of the followers of Husayn's father, Ali, walked in and saluted Muawiya. He listened to the dying caliph drown in self-praise. To that, he recited a verse of his own:

Every charm shall fade at the hands of death.

The eighteen-year rule of the first Umayyad caliph would finally come to an end. However, it was far from over for the ever-expanding Umayyad rule. The Umayyad empire continued to grow through the deserts of northern Africa and beyond the mountains of Persia. Muawiya could not take any of the spoils of his conquests to the grave, but he did pass the inheritance of his rule to his son – the wanton Umayyad prince Yazid.

Yazid was known for his promiscuous and over-indulgent lifestyle. He did not shy away from it either. While his father Muawiya was known for his shrewdness and maintained an aura of piety in the public eye, no matter how superficial, Yazid did not care for the façade. He did not shy away from showing off his fondness of wine, luxury, women, and exotic animals. Now, he would be taking on the task of being the Caliph of the Muslims, which he gladly welcomed.

Yazid was not present in Damascus when his father died, however. Instead, he was on a hunting trip outside of the city, enjoying the company of some questionable friends, music, and too much wine to drink.

Interrupting the party, the messenger from the Umayyad palace rode swiftly into the woods where they hunted. The messenger jumped off his horse and knelt before the drunken Yazid, who was laughing with his friends; they too enjoyed glasses of wine in their hands. The friend playing on the musical instrument nearby stopped his song.

"Master Yazid, I come with news from the palace," the messenger said.

With a look of concern, Yazid replied, "What is it? What happened?"

The messenger handed Yazid a sealed letter. It was from al-Dahhak ibn Qays, one of the regents appointed by his father to ensure the succession of Yazid along with the Umayyad general Muslim ibn Uqba. Al-Dahhak was one of the earliest supporters of Muawiya's rise to power. As Muawiya's former chief of police, and commander of his infantry at the Battle of Siffin, Al-Dahhak was now the governor of Damascus. His letter to Yazid shared condolences for his father's passing along with congratulations for his new rule.

Come to Damascus at once, sir. Your throne awaits you.

Yazid set out to Damascus immediately. He was grieved by his father's demise and did not care to wear a turban or strap a sword to his waist. With disheveled and dusty hair, he threw himself on his father's grave.

The messenger brought forth a letter that punctured my heart, father!

He promised his father he would carry out his work in pummeling his enemies and fulfilling his grandfather's dreams of dominion. Yazid set out for the Green Palace of Damascus to make his first inaugural address as the new caliph of the Muslim empire.

The people were gathered to hear the address of the new caliph. Most were not fond of him. His reputation was known across the empire. Imprudent, impatient, indulgent, and far from regality or any kind of gracefulness, Yazid was not liked.

"Muawiya will be summoned by God for his ill choice for a successor!" were the words of some of the nobles.

It was the unpredictability of Yazid that many detested. With Muawiya, they knew what they were getting. Loyalty to the Umayyads under Muawiya translated into economic prosperity, posts of influence, and luxury. Yazid was a wildcard. People waited.

Yazid entered the Green Palace with his entourage of aides and advisors, most of whom were his father's. Yazid was dressed in silk from head to toe. His turban glittered with beads of gold and his fingers were dressed in rings holding gemstones of all kinds. The glittery monarch reluctantly climbed the pulpit and sat down. The people stared on with watchful eyes. A minute passed, maybe even two. Yazid said nothing. Beads of sweat ran down his forehead.

Al-Dahhak, who was sitting beside him on a lower platform, nervously stood up and turned to Yazid.

"Master," Al-Dahhak began to speak.

"What is it, ibn Qays?" Yazid shot back sharply.

"You must speak to the people," Al-Dahhak advised in a quiet yet firm voice. "They are waiting to give you allegiance. Take it. It is yours."

"I know what is mine," Yazid said as he looked at the crowd. Al-Dahhak bowed his head before him. Yazid adjusted himself in his seat. He took a deep breath and he spoke.

Praise is to God. He does what He wants, and He refrains from whatever He wants. He demeans whomsoever He wants to demean and exalts whomsoever He wants to exalt. Know that, the Commander of the Faithful Muawiya was a rope from the ropes of God. As long as He liked, God maintained that rope and when He desired, He cut it off. He was lesser than his predecessors and he was better than his successors. I shall not complain to God of why he died. Thus, if He forgives him, it shall be through His mercy. If He punishes him, it would be because of his sins. After him I have become entitled to the caliphate. Thus, I neither seek excuse for my ignorance and nor desire to become knowledgeable. You continue on your

way and I will continue on mine. If God does not like some-
thing, He will destroy it and if He likes something, He shall
keep it.

The people turned to each other, unsure of what to make of
it. After some moments, Yazid then made an announcement that
would rally the people of Syria like nothing else. He knew well
the people of Iraq opposed his rule, like they had with his father.
He would not waste time. He declared war.

"We will be going to battle with the people of Iraq. Blood will
flow like a river. Good fortune will be yours," Yazid told his people.

The Syrians cheered. His countrymen pledged allegiance and
vowed to go to battle for him just as they did in Siffin alongside
his father Muawiya against Ali ibn Abi Talib.

Syria was naturally the stronghold of the Umayyad caliph and
Iraq stood as its adversary. Mecca and Medina, however, were
not clearly under Yazid's control. Yazid was adamant on quickly
exerting his control and continuing his father's legacy of dominion. Medina was home to Husayn ibn Ali and Abdullah ibn
Zubayr. If they did not pay allegiance to the new caliphate, Yazid
would not be able to consolidate his power and his rule would
surely be weakened.

Yazid ordered his governor in Medina, Walid ibn Uqba, to
quickly summon the two men and have them pay allegiance to
the new caliphate.

"If they refuse, take their heads. The people should know that their fate will be the same if they do not pay allegiance to me," Yazid ordered coldly.

His brash approach was contrary to that of his father, Muawiya, who used stealthier tactics such as bribes, blackmail, and political allyships. Yazid was not interested in politics as much as he was in pure comination. If they do not fall in line, kill them – that was his modus operandi.

One of Yazid's messengers was dispatched to deliver by hand the caliph's official letter of instruction to take allegiance from the chiefs of Medina, namely Husayn ibn Ali and Abdullah ibn Zubayr, by force if necessary. When the messenger arrived at the governor's home, the sun had set and the governor had retired into his personal chamber. The messenger was told to come back tomorrow by the guard at the governor's door. He refused to leave and told the guard it was an urgent matter.

"What is your matter?" the guard asked.

"I have a letter to personally deliver to the governor."

"You can give it to me."

"My instructions are to hand deliver this letter myself."

The guard replied plainly, "Then it can wait until tomorrow, I have strict orders that governor is not to be disturbed."

"I am not leaving until I deliver this order!" the messenger shouted, "My orders come directly from the caliph himself!"

A stare-down ensued between the two dutiful men. The guard finally gave in and said, "Stay here." He entered the residence and told the governor of the messenger's presence.

"Have him come in," Walid said with a look of concern.

The messenger entered, placed his hand on his chest with a slight bow of the head, and handed the sealed letter to the governor. As the governor read the letter, his eyes widened. Muawiya was dead. Yazid was the new caliph. Husayn would be executed if he did not pay him allegiance. And he, Walid, is responsible to see this through? Walid was overwhelmed and deeply disturbed by the thought of how this all would unfold. "Even Muawiya did not have such a heavy-handed approach", he thought to himself. He did not know what to do.

"Go on and send word to Marwan ibn al-Hakam to come here at once," Walid ordered one of his men.

Marwan arrived at the governor's residence that night. He found Walid with his face buried in his hands, moaning at the tribulation of the news he had received.

"What bemoans you in the middle of the night, cousin?" Marwan asked, more annoyed than concerned.

"Muawiya is dead," Walid said without looking up from his hands.

"What? Are you certain?" Marwan was shocked.

Distraught, Walid handed him Yazid's letter. "See for yourself," he said to Marwan as he looked away.

Marwan studied the letter.

"What do I do, Marwan? Tell me what am I to do?"

"It is simple, cousin," Marwan replied as he continued to study the letter. "You must send a messenger at once and order them to give allegiance to Yazid. If they do it, accept from them and if they refuse, kill them before they receive the news of Muawiya's demise."

"But how can we…" Walid interrupted, but Marwan continued.

"If they know that Muawiya has died, they will rise up and make their own claims to the throne of the caliphate. They will rally the people around them and against the Umayyads. At that point, I fear for your fate cousin. You will not be able to bear what they will do to you."

"What am I to do? What am I to do?" Walid moaned.

"I know that Husayn ibn Ali will never give the oath of allegiance to Yazid ibn Muawiya," Marwan paused. "By God, if I were you, I would not waste the utterance of a word with that man. I would take his head regardless of what he chooses to do."

Walid was not an angel. He was not innocent of the Umayyad legacy and its crimes. He shared in their corruption. But this task was too great for him.

"Alas, if only Walid had not come into the world and had not been worthy of mention," Walid lamented himself.

"Do not complicate this matter and overwhelm your simple mind," Marwan mocked Walid. "These are the sons of Abu Talib. They have not changed, and neither have we. They have been our enemies and always will be. They are the killers of our cousin Uthman and the enemies of the Commander of the Faithful Muawiya…"

"Enough, Marwan! Enough! You know they are the children of Fatima and what remains of the Prophet," Walid shouted and shook his head.

Marwan nodded and smiled, "We are all the same in the end cousin. Call them to come now before you bring about your own demise. You called me here for my counsel and this is what I advise."

Walid reluctantly obliged. He sent one of his servants to summon Husayn and Abdullah ibn Zubayr in the middle of the night. After receiving the message from the governor to come to his residence, Husayn prepared himself for the encounter. He turned to some of the men in his family who were with him at home and told them to accompany him on this visit. While they got ready, Husayn performed *ghusl*, the ritual bath, prayed and supplicated to his Lord.

Arriving at the door of the governor's residence, Husayn turned to his men and told them to wait for him outside.

"I am going inside. If I call for you or you hear me shout, then come in immediately," Husayn instructed solemnly. His family members nodded, hands gripping the handle of their swords, ready to sacrifice for their Imam. Husayn smiled at his brave knights and told them he would not be long. The night was dark, but the stars would shine bright in Arabia's desert sky.

Husayn entered the residence and was escorted to the interior chamber of the governor by one of the guards. Inside, he found the governor waiting for him, along with Marwan seated a short distance away from him. There was tension in the room. Husayn could feel it. Walid and Marwan were not entirely fond of each other and Husayn knew that. In the spirit of goodness, he offered a piece of brotherly advice.

"Maintaining amity is better than discord and peace is better than mischief. Now is the time for you to remain united, may the Almighty Allah make peace between you," Husayn advised. But they did not respond. Silence remained. After a few moments, Husayn asked about Muawiya.

"Have you received some news about Muawiya? We know he was sick, and his illness had prolonged for some time. What is his condition now?" Husayn asked inquisitively.

Walid could hold himself no longer.

"*Athamallah Ujoorakum!*" Walid shouted. "May the Almighty reward you for your patience in the calamity of Muawiya's passing!"

Husayn did not respond right away.

"I know he was a sincere uncle for you," Walid half-heartedly said. "And now he is gone!" The theatrics did not impress Husayn.

"We are for God and to Him we return," Husayn solemnly replied as he watched Walid fiddle with the letter in his hands.

"This is the letter from the Commander of the Faithful, Yazid," Walid said still looking at the letter in hand.

Commander of the Faithful Yazid? The title was odd enough when used before the name of Muawiya. Now the governor recited it before the name of the unruly Umayyad son? Husayn remembered as a little boy how his grandfather, the Prophet, gave his father Ali that title.

"You are the Commander of the Faithful, O Ali. Through you the believers are known after me." The Prophet held no one else in such regard. Husayn witnessed this from his grandfather's lap.

"Why have you called me here now?"

"To pay allegiance," the governor said coldly.

"I will not give allegiance in secret," Husayn replied sharply. "Nor shall allegiance taken in secret be accepted. When you go out to the public to take allegiance, call me with the people and it shall be done the same for all."

Husayn had a clear responsibility to the religion and its people. Truth was not to be kept in the dark, nor was it to be toyed with at the whims of tyrants. In the hearts of the pure, the truth was clear. But with the works of these tyrants, the ordinary person may not be able to decipher it. Husayn's God-given role was to make that truth clear, to remind the people of the principles and values that his grandfather lived and died for. The nation of Muhammad would not be forsaken, so long as his disciples were amongst them.

Walid nodded in agreement.

"Apologies Husayn, you are right. It is late. We can discuss this further tomorrow." The governor gave Husayn leave and apologized again for the trouble. Marwan could not believe it. As Husayn was about to make his exit from the chamber, Marwan stood up frantically and unabashedly reprimanded the governor.

"If this man leaves here without giving you his oath of allegiance, you will never get it from him!" Marwan screamed. Husayn turned away from the doors and looked back at the Umayyad chiefs, while Marwan continued, "Seize him at once and make him pay allegiance to Yazid. And if he does not, you should have his head!"

"O son of the freed slaves! Who will kill me? You or him? You only lie, and courage does not come from the likes of you." Husayn roared and the sheep fell back in his chair. Marwan did not respond. He knew his place. Husayn turned to the governor and made his position clear.

"Governor, you know who we are. We are the Family of Prophethood. Our home is the place of God's angels and the House of Revelation. God started his creation with us, and He will end it with us. As for Yazid, we know who he is. He is a murderer, a drunkard transgressor, a debased man who commits crimes openly without regard to anything or anyone. A person like me does not give allegiance to a person like him. We will see what the morning brings."

Husayn walked out. Walid did not object. Marwan was livid. "You fool! What good is my counsel if you don't listen to it? You will never get this opportunity again." Marwan scolded Walid.

Walid had been moved by Husayn's words. He had somewhat of a change of heart and at least in those moments, challenged Marwan's audacity.

"Woe be to you. Your counsel would bring me to destroy my own faith. By God, if I were given all the world's wealth and dominion over everything, to kill Husayn – I would not. Are you mad? Should I kill Husayn because he said he will not pay Yazid allegiance? The man who stands before God on the Day of Judgment, with Husayn's blood on his hands, will face a terrible end."

Marwan scoffed. "Sure. Makes sense. You made the right decision," he sarcastically said.

As Husayn returned home with his men, he looked at the day ahead and what was to come. He knew he had to leave Medina. Before embarking on his eventual journey to the lands of Iraq, Husayn would visit Mecca for the very last time.

The next morning, Husayn found Marwan outside of his house. Kicking the sand, it seemed like he had been waiting out there for some time. When he saw Husayn, he rejoiced.

"Master Husayn, I am your well-wisher," Marwan said with a half-smile. "Listen to what I have to say, it is truly for your well-being and safety."

Husayn was not convinced. "What do you want, Marwan?" he replied in short.

"I recommend that you reconsider your position from last night. Pay allegiance to Yazid. There is good in it for you, both in this life and the next," Marwan asserted.

Husayn was patient with him long enough. Marwan was the son of one of the Prophet's staunchest enemies, a man named al-Hakam. The Prophet exiled al-Hakam in the Muslims' bloodless takeover of Mecca from the chiefs of Quraysh in 630 AD. The staunch opponent of the Prophet lived in exile in a nearby town called Taif for over ten years, until he was pardoned when his nephew Uthman came into power several years later. Like many in the Umayyad clan, Marwan and his family went from being exiled by the Prophet to assuming government posts and amassing wealth and influence during the Uthman administration. The audacity of Marwan was so contemptible; it saw even his own friends despise him. Husayn now turned to Marwan completely and again put him in his place with words that were a sermon in their own right:

> If the community accepts a ruler as debased as Yazid, then farewell to Islam. Your counsel to me is to pledge allegiance to Yazid who does not shy away from transgression? What you say is so absurd. But such is to be expected from you. You are such an accursed man that the Holy Prophet had damned you when you were in the loins of your father. So, leave me, Marwan. You are the enemy of God and His Prophet! We are the family of God's Prophet. The truth comes from us alone. We are with it, and it is with us. I heard the Prophet say, 'The caliphate is unlawful for the family of Abu Sufyan,' whom he called 'the freed slaves and sons of freed slaves'. My grandfather said, 'O people, when you see Muawiya on my pulpit, kill him.' By God, the people of Medina

saw the man on the pulpit of my grandfather, and they did nothing.

Husayn turned away from Marwan and began to walk. Marwan ran up to him and stood in his way.

"By God! You will not leave from here until you pledge allegiance to Yazid! You shall do so submissively. I know what you, the family of Ali, hold in your hearts of malice to the family of Abu Sufyan! You hate them and they are right in seeing you as their enemies." Marwan was breathing heavily. His eyes were bulging, his face was red. Husayn stood tall before Marwan and shot back.

I said get away from me, you vile man! I am from the purified family of the Prophet. God said, 'He only desires to keep away the filth from you, O people of the House! And to purify you a thorough purification.' Glad tidings to you for possessing everything that the Holy Prophet despised. You will meet my grandfather before our Lord, and there you shall know of my right and the right of Yazid.

Husayn walked past Marwan and continued on his way. Marwan was burning inside. He did not wait a moment further before sending word to Damascus to let Yazid know what had transpired, from Walid's weakness before Husayn to his own encounter with the Imam. Yazid was outraged. "A person like him does not pay allegiance to a person like me? Who does he think he is?", Yazid swore that he would not wait any longer before he would have Husayn's head. He made that clear in his next letter to the governor of Medina. His letter said in part:

> From the Servant of God, the Commander of the Faithful Yazid, to Walid ibn Uqbah.
>
> When this letter of mine reaches you, you are to command the people of Medina to pledge allegiance to me. Do not worry about Abdullah ibn Zubayr. Leave him alone. He cannot escape us. As for Husayn ibn Ali, his severed head must accompany your reply to me. If you do that, you will have endless rewards from me.

When Walid received the letter, Husayn had already left his home and was on his way to Mecca. Before Husayn would leave, however, he would say his last farewell at the grave of his grandfather, Muhammad.

CHAPTER 5

FAREWELL, GRANDFATHER

I have not come to create mischief nor to oppress. Rather, I seek only to bring reform to the nation of my grandfather, the Prophet of God.

– Husayn ibn Ali

Husayn's heart was heavy, not merely for the challenges ahead, but for the goodbyes he was about to give. He walked slowly to the grave of his grandfather, a place he had frequented ever since he was a child. He was not only leaving this sanctuary of his behind, he was also leaving the city that he grew up in and in which he had built so many memories. This is where he used to run up to his grandfather, Muhammad, and jump into his lap while the Prophet advised his companions. This is where he would pray beside his mother, Fatima, and hold hands in supplication. This is where he followed his father, Ali, and accompanied him on his trips to the marketplace and the mosque. This is where he played with his older brother, Hasan and younger sister, Zaynab.

Though the Prophet, Fatima, Ali, and Hasan were all gone, Medina was still home for Husayn. But he could stay home no longer. There was a journey of tribulation and sacrifice ahead. That to him would be clear. As he walked towards the grave of his grandfather, his mission was simple, just as it always had

been – to protect the faith and the faithful. He submitted to the
will of God, to whatever challenges he would face ahead, without
a shadow of doubt or hesitation. In every moment, with every
stride and in every breath, that is what Husayn would do.

Husayn kneeled before the grave of his grandfather and began to pray. He looked towards the heavens and raised his hands
in supplication to God.

> Dear Lord, this is the grave of your beloved prophet Mu-
> hammad. I am the son of his daughter, the Lady Fat-
> ima. What has befallen us is well known to you. Dear
> Lord, I love what is good and abhor what is evil. You
> are the one with all glory and greatness. So, I pray to you
> by the right of the one who is buried in this blessed grave.
> I ask that you lead me to what shall bring your pleasure
> and the pleasure of your Prophet.

The heavy-hearted Husayn touched his grandfather's grave
with his palm. He gently brushed the top of it as tears fell down
his cheek. Moments of silent contemplation passed as he gazed
at the grave thinking of his late grandfather. Husayn was a young
boy, only five or six years old, when Muhammad died. He
thought of those days. He missed his grandfather's embrace. He
missed running up to his grandfather and jumping into his lap
as he spoke with his companions. He always greeted him with
his wide-open arms and joyous smile. He never turned him
away. Instead, he would seat him on his knee and tell his companions a profound statement:

Husayn is of me, and I am of him. God loves those who love Husayn.

Husayn could never forget the kindness of his eyes and the glowing aura of his face. It was not merely the love of a grandfather: it was the love of God through His most beloved prophet. That love shined on him every day, through the Prophet's radiant face.

Husayn was reminded of the Prophet's face daily, even in this much later part of his life. The blessing was due to his own son, Ali al-Akbar. Husayn's eldest son was said to look so much like the Prophet Muhammad that people would just stare at him in awe uninterrupted. Everyone in the family gazed at Ali al-Akbar, especially when they missed their grandfather, Muhammad.

Husayn prayed. He cried. The heaviness in his heart would not subside. The nation of his grandfather had gone so astray that the likes of Yazid would sit on the Prophet's pulpit. It pained Husayn what the nation had come to. His complaint, however, was only to God. As Husayn continued to pray and lament to his Lord, he briefly fell asleep.

It is said that in that brief sleep before dawn, Husayn saw his grandfather Muhammad in a dream. The Prophet came before him with a group of heavenly angels to his right and left. The Prophet took his grandson Husayn into his arms for a warm embrace. Husayn smiled and held his grandfather tight. The Prophet too smiled. He kissed Husayn on the forehead and placed his hands on his shoulders. His smile disappeared.

My son, Husayn, your tragedy is near. Soon you will be killed in Karbala by a group from my nation. Your head will be severed. They will kill you while you are thirsty. They will refuse to give you even a drop of water. Despite these crimes, they will expect our intercession on the Day of Reckoning. For them, no such intercession will be given. My dear Husayn, I am eager to see you. Your father, mother, and brother have come to me. They too are eager to see you. You will come back to us soon.

Husayn awoke from his dream, still seated at his grandfather's grave. He was comforted by the Prophet's embrace. He knew the time was near. His fate was clear. He could not leave Medina without also visiting his mother's grave. She had died so soon after the Prophet. Husayn would never forget that year of sorrow for him and his siblings. They were such young, delicate children, enduring the loss of their grandfather Muhammad and mother, Fatima, within a few short months. The tragedy was unbearable for any ordinary individual, let alone a child. But this family was far from ordinary. They were raised to give, to sacrifice. All that they had was given for the sake of God. Husayn knew that. He too would give his all, for the sake of God, for the sake of the faith, for the sake of his nation, the nation of Muhammad.

Husayn cried at his mother's grave what seemed to be endless tears. They were tears for her sacrifice, for her unrelenting strength in the face of oppression, for her dedication to God and the faith, for all that she gave to preserve the message of her father, the Prophet Muhammad. Husayn cried. His grief could not be contained. The memories of her last days filled his mind and the pain overwhelmed his heart.

Mother Fatima, please speak to me. Please, mother.

He remembered pleading with her the day that she passed, after her soul had departed her body. He remembered how his father, Ali, sobbed so intensely as he embraced him and his brother Hasan.

Husayn said his farewell at his mother's grave, though it was so hard to leave. He went on to see his brother Hasan's grave nearby. He always looked up to his older brother, the Imam before him, and the leader of the family after their father was assassinated in Kufa almost two decades earlier. They both endured much after the father's death, especially the pain of abdicating the caliphate to Muawiya. It was not relinquishing power that hurt them, but rather witnessing the erosion of the nation's moral fabric. Abdication of the caliphate came by way of Hasan's peace accord with Muawiya. Though some looked at it as a victory for the Umayyads, Hasan had strategically saved the faith through his sacrifice. He laid the groundwork for what Husayn was now moving towards. A few years after the peace accord, Hasan would be poisoned at the hands of his wife, Juda. Muawiya had promised her to be wed to his own son and a life of riches if she carried out the evil deed. She did not fare as well as she thought, as Muawiya was not keen on keeping promises, especially once he got what he wanted.

Husayn recalled the conversation he had on his brother's deathbed, after days of Hasan suffering from the poison that had spread throughout his body. In his last moments with his brother, Husayn cried. Hasan made a request of him:

"Do not cry for me, my brother," said Hasan.

"How can I not cry over this great tragedy, my brother?" Husayn said as he wiped away his flowing tears.

"Save your tears. Your tragedy will be greater. For there will be no day like your day, Husayn."

That day was finally near. He poured water over his brother's grave and sent his peace and blessings upon him. "I will see you soon my brother." Husayn returned home to tell his family that they would be leaving Medina at once.

When Husayn came home, his family had been anticipating his arrival. As he entered through the front door, they anxiously stood by for his orders. The women and children were gathered. They knew that the time would come, but when, they were not certain.

"We are leaving Medina," he said simply.

The room quickly filled with grief.

"Must we leave the city of our grandfather?" the children cried.

"This is our home, to leave is so painful," the women wept. Husayn embraced them and asked them to be strong and have patience for the long journey ahead.

Husayn's half-brother Muhammad came to the house as soon as he heard of his brother's plans to leave the city. Muhammad ibn al-Hanafiyya (named after his mother Khawlah bint Jafar who was known as al-Hanafiyya) was born in 637 AD, a few years after Lady Fatima tragically died. It is said that Fatima was very direct in her will to her husband Imam Ali. She asked him to marry after her and make sure her children were to be cared for. She asked Ali to raise sons, brothers to Husayn, to support Husayn in his great sacrifice. Ali would do as she asked. Husayn would have his brothers, ones who would come to his aid at every call.

When Muhammad arrived at Husayn's home, he found it filled with wails and cries. Not much was said. The tears spoke for themselves. It was understood. Husayn's brother Muhammad joined them in lamentation, unable to hold back his own tears. He went up to his older brother and embraced him tight, kissed his hand, and looked up with his teary eyes. The women and children watched as the two brothers stood at the center of the room. Muhammad wiped away his tears and asked Husayn for permission to speak candidly. Husayn amicably granted him that.

> My brother Husayn, I wish I could be sacrificed for you. You are the most beloved person in this world to me. You are my soul. You are my life. You are the one I trust and the one I obey. God has chosen you as our leader and you are of the chiefs of Paradise. I desire to offer a perspective, perhaps a small piece of advice for what lies ahead, if you allow me.

Muhammad paused. Husayn nodded. His brother continued.

> *Do stay away from paying allegiance to Yazid ibn
> Muawiya. Also stay away from the places of mischief
> and conflict. Send your messengers to the people and
> monitor the situation further. If they give allegiance to
> you, well and good. If they begin to support someone
> else, God has not lessened your faith nor taken away any
> virtue from you. My brother, I dread that you may go to
> one of these towns where people are intent on creating
> conflict. One group may support you while another will
> oppose you. When this happens, they will fight one an-
> other, and you will be the first to receive their spears and
> arrows. I could not bear to see the most virtuous of
> God's creation be humiliated as such.*

Husayn heard the sincerity in his voice. "Where do you suggest
that I should go brother?" he asked him.

> *Go to Mecca and stay there if you find peace. If not, go
> to Yemen, turn to the deserts and mountains and go
> from town to town away from the people's mischief.
> That way you will see what destiny brings while you are
> safe from the people. Your intention would be best and
> your work would be done in a way we can foresee. This
> is a safer approach, and you will not risk needing to
> abandon your mission for the faith.*

Husayn put his hands on his brother's shoulders and reassured him that there was no abandoning of this mission. The
faith would be preserved, and God's message protected. "My

brother, even if there is not a single place of safety in this whole world for us, I will never give allegiance to Yazid."

Muhammad wept. He could not hold back his cries. His body would shake. It was hard for him to stand. Husayn embraced him and comforted him.

"My brother, thank you for your sincerity. I am going to Mecca. My brothers and nephews will be accompanying me. Do not worry. You can stay here in Medina and keep me informed of its affairs." Husayn left a letter for his brother before he left Medina. From this letter, Husayn's intentions were made clear as day. His motivation was simple, and his determination was unwavering.

> *In the name of God, the Beneficent the Merciful,*
>
> *This is the will of Husayn ibn Ali to his brother, Muhammad ibn al-Hanafiyah.*
>
> *Husayn testifies that there is no god but God and He has no partner or equal to Him; and that Muhammad is His Servant and His Messenger who has come from Him with truth; and that Paradise is true and Hellfire is true and the Day of Reckoning will come... I have not gone out to celebrate or rejoice over what I possess. I have not come to create mischief nor to oppress. Rather, I seek only to bring reform to the nation of my grandfather, the Prophet of God. I wish to enjoin what is good and prevent what is evil. I wish to guide the affairs of our people just like my grandfather Muhammad and father, Ali. The one who accepts me with truth should know*

*that truth is with God. As for those who stand against
me, I will remain patient. God will judge between us,
surely He is the best of judges.*

*This is what I leave for you, my brother. I have no suc-
cess except from God. I rely on Him and to Him I return.*

Husayn and his family left for Mecca to seek refuge in the Kaaba.
The men, women, and children were gathered in this caravan of
sorrow, far from eager to leave their home. As the caravan
moved, the children would look back at the City of the Prophet.
Husayn too would look back at it and give yet another farewell
to his grandfather, mother, and brother. He looked towards
Mecca now and prayed to God: "My Lord, deliver me from the
unjust people."

CHAPTER 6

AT THE HOUSE OF GOD

What do you say about a people that threaten the life of the Prophet's only remaining grandson? That they design for him not to find peace or take refuge in any town or land?

– Husayn ibn Ali

The birds of Mecca flew overhead, casting a shadow over the caravan of Husayn as it entered God's city. Some watched as the caravan passed them by, wary of what was to come. Others leaped forward in excitement at having the honor of his presence amongst them.

"It is the grandson of the Prophet! It is Husayn!" Pilgrims and locals alike flocked towards them as word spread in the city that Husayn had come to Mecca.

Mecca held a special place in Husayn's heart. It was the epicenter of higher consciousness. The city developed over the centuries around the house of God, the Kaaba. The Kaaba itself was built by Husayn's prophetic ancestors – Abraham and his sons. As the grandson of the Prophet Muhammad, Husayn's lineage went back to the very beginning of prophetic messages. God was always the center of life. This was a reality so simple, yet so beautiful, for it is God who takes life and God who gives it. Surely, God brought life through His House. For in the House of God,

Husayn's father, Ali ibn Abi Talib, was born. No other person in history had that honor. Husayn came from that. He was the son of that same Ali who entered Mecca and reclaimed it for the worship of the one true God. Husayn's father would ascend on the shoulders of the Prophet and destroy the idols of Quraysh that for years had infested the Kaaba. In 630 AD, the Prophet Muhammad and Imam Ali captured Mecca in a bloodless conquest, ending the battles between the Muslims and the pagans of Quraysh.

At that time, Quraysh was led by Abu Sufyan, Yazid's grandfather. He was the staunchest enemy of the Prophet. Abu Sufyan had gone to battle against him time and time again. He swore to kill Muhammad, but to no avail. The Prophet, however, did lose many of his dearest friends and relatives in these battles launched by Quraysh. The Prophet saw his brave uncle Hamza ibn Abd al-Muttalib killed in the Battle of Uhud. Hamza was one of the chief warriors in the Muslim army and a great defender of the Prophet. Hamza had killed Abu Sufyan's father-in-law, Utba ibn Rabiah, in the Battle of Badr in the year prior. Abu Sufyan's wife, Hind, swore vengeance. She wanted to be present at Uhud to make sure that Hamza would be killed.

Hind's servant, Wahshi, was tasked with one thing and one thing alone – to kill Hamza. For that, Wahshi would be rewarded without measure. The servant of Hind waited for the right moment to strike. During the battle, chaos had ensued when the rearguard of the Muslim army left their ranks to seek war booty. The Prophet was left exposed and the threat on his life was imminent. Ali and Hamza came to his defense, fending off the scores of enemies that now surrounded Muhammad. While Hamza was fighting several Meccan warriors at once, Hind's servant found his chance. Wahshi lifted his javelin, a light spear he had trained with, and threw it as hard as he could. He managed to strike Hamza in the chest. Hamza would fall martyr on the battlefield of Uhud.

Even though the Battle of Uhud was a stalemate, as the Meccans were not able to invade or take over Medina, the Muslims were dealt a heavy blow. They lost so many of their men that day – a total of 85 martyrs. It was not enough for the revenge-seeking families of Quraysh to see those men die. Hind celebrated that day along with other women from Quraysh by mutilating the bodies of the fallen Muslim soldiers. Hind sat at Hamza's body and rejoiced. She took out her knife and gauged out Hamza's liver. She took a bite out of the liver, chewed it, and spit it out. She proceeded to make a necklace out of his mutilated body parts like the other women. Dressing her servant Wahshi with the horrific necklace she had made, she stood up and shouted into the desert plain that was covered with corpses.

We have paid you back for Badr

a battle that follows a battle is always violent.

I could not bear the loss of Utbah

nor my brother and his uncle and my first-born.

I have slaked my vengeance and fulfilled my vow.

O' Wahshi, you have quieted the burning in my chest.

I shall thank Wahshi as long as I live,

until my bones rot in the grave.

The Prophet and his fellow Muslims mourned Hamza. He was honored with the title of 'the Master of Martyrs', and he continued to be called that. Abu Sufyan was Yazid's grandfather. Hind was his grandmother. Their spite for the Prophet and his family was passed down as their tribe's, the Umayyads', badge of honor. They prided themselves on this enmity and animosity against *Banu Hashim*, the Prophet's clan. No matter what victory they claimed for themselves, whether it be by Hind and her killing of Hamza, her son Muawiya in his rise to power, or Yazid in his inheriting of the caliphate, it was simply not enough. Hate remained in their hearts for Muhammad, as he changed the order of their society and way of life in Mecca with the advent of Islam. Now, Husayn was challenging the abhorrent status quo by not paying allegiance to Yazid's caliphate. It would not be coincidence that Husayn would end up sharing the same title and an even more egregious fate as his great uncle, at the hands of the same people.

Even with all that ensued in the years of attacks on the Muslims and the lives lost in battles, the Prophet freed their conquered opponents and gave them a path forward to start new lives in the all-encompassing community of God. "You are free." Perhaps that benevolence made some members of Quraysh even more resentful. Abu Sufyan and his people remained bitter, spiteful, and bent on vengeance for what they had lost. "If we cannot destroy Islam from the outside, we will destroy it from the inside." This was the promise of Abu Sufyan to his sons.

Muawiya made it his life's calling. Yazid wanted to carry on his father's legacy.

Half a century had passed from the conquest of Mecca in 630 AD. The previous two decades saw the rule of the family of the very man that was the Prophet's gravest enemy. Though they were freed by the Prophet, many people had forgotten the history or chose to ignore it and instead to create their own interpretation of the events that transpired in the growing Muslim nation. Some had strayed so much from reality that they were on the verge of skewing Islam to an unredeemable distortion. Husayn would remind them of the truth with everything he had, even if it would cost him his life in the very end.

Yazid's governor in Mecca, Amr ibn Saeed, had gotten word that Husayn was likely to come to Mecca after departing Medina. Upon Husayn's arrival in Mecca, Amr did not waste any time before going to Husayn and asking him directly about his plans in Mecca.

Amr found the grandson of the Prophet at the Kaaba with some of his family members and a group of pilgrims that sought the Imam out for guidance. Amr was already troubled by the scene. Not a day has passed and Husayn was already gaining followers and had a constant company of admirers. People gravitated towards him. Amr grew agitated by the possibility of Husayn's growing influence in the city he governed.

"What has brought you to Mecca, Husayn?" Amr asked bluntly as he stood before the imam, interrupting the pilgrims' questions.

Husayn smiled. "I have come for God and the sanctuary of His House," he said as he looked at the magnanimous Kaaba. Amr scoffed and walked away. Husayn continued on with the pilgrims.

The news of Husayn's decision to refuse Yazid was spreading. Those who reflected saw Husayn's refusal as a stance of honor – not one of vainglory in a struggle for power. They knew Husayn was above that. He and his family had sacrificed for decades to protect the sanctity of Islam and maintain unity in the young Muslim nation. Husayn was receiving letters of support from different parts of the nation that heard he refused to pay allegiance to Yazid, especially from the people of Iraq.

Amr wrote a letter to Yazid informing him of Husayn's presence in Mecca and his growing popularity. He warned of Husayn's threat to the Umayyads. Yazid did not need any direction when it came to his suspicions of Husayn. His spite guided him in that. Yazid wrote to Husayn's cousin, Abdullah ibn Abbas. Abdullah was close to Husayn's father, Ali, and was a senior in the family.

> *Your cousin, Husayn, and the enemy of Allah, Ibn Zubayr, have refused to pledge allegiance to me. They have gone to Mecca, and they intend to spread mischief. Know that they have put themselves in mortal danger. I will have Zubayr killed by the sword. As for Husayn, I wish to excuse him as he is part of your family. Word has come to me that the Shia of Iraq write to him, and he writes back to them. It seems that they are promising the caliphate, while he promises to lead them.*

Our families have deep ties. For what reasons has Husayn cut off these relations and severed these ties? You are the leader of your tribe and chief of your community. So, go forth and meet with Husayn. Speak to him and restrain him from this mischief.

If you can stop him from his campaign, we will give him security and honor. I will give Husayn the same that my father gave his brother. And if he wants more, I can guarantee whatever he desires. You both can have whatever you like. With this, I give you my word.... Make haste in your reply to my letter. I wait to read your demands. And peace be upon you.

Abdullah ibn Abbas read between the lines. He knew Yazid was not genuine. As much as Yazid may have not understood Husayn and his movement, Abdullah knew Yazid very well. He knew that Yazid was trying whatever he could to do away with Husayn. He would want nothing more than for him to just disappear. But Husayn, like his brother and father, could not leave the nation. He did not have to be at the helm to lead his people and guide them to God's path. But he had to be present. With all of the trials, tribulations, and injustices he and his family had experienced, they remained part and parcel of their community. That is one of the reasons why he lived in Medina – it was the center of the Muslim nation. Hence why Yazid ordered to have Husayn pay allegiance and be contained so quickly. Husayn, however, thwarted that effort with his move to Mecca for pilgrimage. Abdullah ibn Abbas replied to Yazid.

I received your letter. You have spoken at length of Husayn's and Ibn Zubayr's move to Mecca. As for Ibn Zubayr, we have nothing to do with him. He is absorbed with his own pursuits. Aside from that, we know he conceals his own malice for us like the flint stone conceals fire...

As for Husayn, when he entered Mecca, leaving behind the sanctuary of his grandfather and the house of his father, I asked him about his mission. He informed me that your officials in Medina harassed him and spoke to him without regard. Therefore, he came to me and took refuge in the sanctuary of God here in Mecca. I shall meet with him about the things you have written to me. I will not refrain from giving good counsel, so that God will bring unity to our nation and put out the fire of discord. May God keep the blood of the nation safe.

I say, have fear of God – both openly and in secret. Do not be one to offend the Muslims or position yourself in a way ready to ambush and oppress them. Do not wish to dig a pit for them, because those who dig a pit for others will surely fall into it themselves. There are many who are hopeful, but who do not fulfill their desires. I advise that you choose for yourself a lifestyle of reciting the Quran and spreading the tradition of the Prophet.

Engage in fasting and praying, to help you on this path, so that the vain pastimes of the world and sinful activities may not hinder you from them. Whatever busies you from Allah will harm you and eventually it will all perish. But whatever consumes you in matters of the Hereafter, it will profit you and it will be everlasting. And may peace be with you.

Yazid was not entirely fond of Abdullah's advice, to say the least. It was not long before Yazid replaced Walid ibn Utba, his governor in Medina, with someone else who would get his work done the way he wanted. Walid was not as heavy-handed as Yazid wanted him to be. He proved that much in allowing Husayn to leave Medina. He replaced Walid with Mecca's governor, Amr ibn Saeed. Amr took to Medina in the month of Ramadan. His objective was to quell any opposition to Yazid and the new administration with an iron fist. The morning after his arrival, he had the people gathered at the Prophet's Mosque and gave a sermon.

Amr was dressed in red from top to bottom. He wrapped a scarlet turban around his head. People watched him as he intently ascended the pulpit. He did not smile. He sat on the pulpit for a few moments. The people stared at him and he stared back. Amr finally broke the silence, but he did not begin in God's name, nor did he send peace upon anyone. He lashed out at the people who gathered below him.

O people of Medina! What is your problem that you stare at me as you do now? Do you wish to slay me with your swords? It seems that you have forgotten what you have done. If revenge had been taken from you in the first instance you would not have repeated it. You were deceived when you killed Uthman. You had in him a patient, forbearing leader. He did not use his anger

*against you, nor did he have an ego to oppress you. Now,
take heed. The leader over you is in his prime. He is
young, his ambitions are great, owns a firm base, and
has the power to do as he wishes. He has a close and
watchful eye over what is taking place in this nation. He
is ready to face it all. Be assured, when he chews something, he will swallow it. And if he kicks something, it
will shatter.*

Amr was so intense in his speech; it is said that his nose began
to bleed. When he noticed the blood running down from his
nose, he stopped and looked out. Someone from the crowd
threw him a turban to wipe away the blood. At that sight, of Amr
wiping his blood with a turban on the Prophet's pulpit, people
gasped.

"This is an evil that will be a sign of our time!" Amr did not
really care to take heed.

While Amr replaced Walid and set the new tone in Medina,
Imam Husayn was being visited by scores of personalities in
Mecca. One particular visit shed light onto Husayn's mindset, as
well as the mindset of his contemporaries. Abdullah ibn Umar
and Abdullah ibn Abbas visited the Imam and shared their
thoughts with him. Ibn Umar was the first to give his opinion.

*O Husayn... You know very well how much the Umay-
yads despise you. Yazid ibn Muawiya rules the nation
now. I think the people will be lured by his promises of
wealth and power, so much so that they will go the
lengths to kill you if you remain a threat to him. And*

*with that, so many people will be killed because of you
in this ordeal. I remember the Prophet himself saying,
'Husayn will be killed. If they kill him, God will degrade
and humiliate them until the Day of Reckoning.' Let us
have an accord instead, so that the people may join in
that peace. Perhaps you can remain patient as you chose
patience with Muawiya and his rule. And God will be
the judge between you and the unjust.*

Husayn listened to Ibn Umar intently. He calmly replied with
a simple question. "Knowing what the Prophet has said, you still
advise that I am to give allegiance to the man and make peace
with him?" Ibn Umar was flustered. Ibn Abbas was of a different
opinion.

"You are right Master Husayn," Ibn Abbas quickly said. "The
Prophet spoke of this during his lifetime. I heard him say, 'May
God remove his mercy from Yazid. He will kill my grandson Husayn. My beloved will be killed by people of my nation. They will
leave him and they will not come to his aid. Their words and
their deeds will be a paradox.'"

Ibn Abbas could not hold himself from crying as he narrated
the Prophet's words. Tears fell from Husayn's eyes as he nodded
his head, reminiscing about his grandfather, Muhammad. The
Prophet of God shared Husayn's fate not only with Husayn and
his family, but he warned his companions and followers of the
inevitable reality that would manifest itself fifty years later.

"You know that I am the son of the Prophet's daughter," Husayn told Ibn Abbas as he continued to cry.

"By God, I know that there is no one else on this Earth that is like you in this regard. It is an obligation for the people of this nation to help you just as it is an obligation for them to pray before their lord and pay alms to the poor. One of these deeds cannot be accepted without the other."

With that response, Husayn paused. He looked off for a few moments. He returned his gaze to Ibn Abbas with pain in his eyes.

What do you say about a people who drove out the son of the Prophet's daughter from his home? Who pushed him away from the sanctuary of his grandfather the Prophet of God? Who made him leave the place the Prophet himself made as a home for his people escaping the persecution of the pagans? What do you say about a people that threaten the life of the Prophet's only remaining grandson? That they design for him not to find peace or take refuge in any town or land? What do you say of the people that are determined to kill the grandson of the Prophet even though he has no crime or sin? They wish to kill him though he has not strayed from the path of his Prophet, nor has he disbelieved in God. What do you say of these people?

Ibn Abbas shook his head and continued to cry as he listened to his cousin's son. He wiped away the tears from his face and spoke from the heart.

Nothing can be said other than these men do not believe in God or His Prophet. They pray only to show off. None of them truly remembers God but a few. They roam around aimlessly with those who do not have a path with God. You are the pride and joy of God's Prophet. I know that God sees what these oppressors do. I say that whoever neglects you or has the audacity to wage war on you, they will not gain a thing... But know that I will sacrifice my life for you. If you were to accept me, I would fight for you with this sword of mine until both my arms are severed. And even at that time, I would not have fulfilled an ounce of your right. I am at your service and awaiting your commands, Master Husayn.

Ibn Umar was growing restless. Before Husayn could respond and acknowledge the words of Ibn Abbas, Ibn Umar interjected.

"Stop this at once and return to Medina, Husayn! You are to make peace for the people. Stay in Medina and do not leave again. There is no benefit for people in what you are doing. If you want, do not even pay allegiance to Yazid. You never know, the man may not live for very long, and God will then show you the way."

Husayn looked Ibn Umar in the eyes and asked him, "Am I guilty in your mind, Abdullah? For if I am in the wrong, then turn me back. I will consent and agree to what you say."

Ibn Umar grew apologetic and tried to explain himself. "By God, of course not! God would not blame the grandson of the Prophet for this, nor would one claim that Yazid ibn Muawiya is equal to Husayn in purity and closeness to God's Prophet." Ibn

Umar sighed. "But I fear that these people will kill you. I fear that no one will come to support you. Come back to Medina with us. Do not even pay allegiance, just stay in your home."

Whether Ibn Umar genuinely believed that the Umayyads would leave Husayn be or he was going on a whim is not for certain. But Husayn knew the Umayyads. He knew what they wanted and what they would do to get it. He made that clear to Ibn Umar.

> *These people will never leave me be. So long as I am alive, they will try everything in their power to get me to pay allegiance. When they cannot, they will put me to death. Abdullah, I ask you, do you know how insignificant this world is for God? One of the oppressors from the Children of Israel brought the severed head of Yahya ibn Zakaria while that head still spoke to them with the words of God. They killed seventy prophets, from dawn to sunset, without hesitation. Thereafter they went back to their markets and carried out their days, as if nothing had happened. God's punishment did not rain down on them immediately, but eventually they could not escape it.*

Abdullah ibn Umar did not have much of a reply. He simply put his head down. He could not convince the Imam, nor was his own conviction strong enough to claim it was the truth. Husayn turned to Ibn Abbas.

> *Ibn Abbas, you are my father's cousin. You spent much time with my father and shared with him good counsel.*

He took your advice and sought your opinion. And you responded in kind with sincere counsel. Now, I ask you to go on to Medina in God's protection. Keep me informed of the developments there. I will make this place my residence until I confirm a positive response from those who wish to help me. When they leave me, I shall select another place. And I swear, by the same words Ibrahim spoke when his people wished to throw him in that great fire, that God is sufficient for me. He is the best of the helpers.

Even when all the odds seemed stacked against him, Husayn did not fret. He had hope. He looked to God, for He was sufficient for him.

CHAPTER 7

HIS AMBASSADOR TO IRAQ

Master Husayn… 18,000 men of Kufa have given their oath of allegiance to you before me. When you receive this letter, come forward, as all the people are waiting for you.

– Muslim ibn Aqeel

When news of Yazid's caliphate reached Iraq, many were opposed to it. There were some who did not care who was at the helm, so long as they filled their coffers with gold and silver. But overall, Iraq had long been the center of support for Husayn's father, Ali. That is where Ali had moved his caliphate (656 – 661 AD) when he ruled the nation. In fact, Ali governed from the city of Kufa. That was the hub of his followers and supporters. It was also in the Mosque of Kufa that Ali was assassinated in 661 AD. With a demoralized army that had no appetite for battle, Hasan ibn Ali gave up power and signed an accord with Muawiya. Though he was the first on the battlefield to face off with Muawiya, he chose the accord as a strategic move to maintain peace, preserve unity in the nation, and ultimately save the religion from being obliterated by the ambitions and the Umayyad hunger for power that knew no bounds.

Muawiya had designs to destroy the faith from the inside, as his father, Abu Sufyan, had directed him and his sons to do, decades earlier. Muawiya did not honor the accord, which guaranteed that all people in the nation, regardless of ethnicity or creed, would be protected by the law. Instead, Muawiya instituted nepotism and marginalized those who were loyal to the Prophet's descendants. Even though Muawiya did not honor the accord, it played a crucial role in exposing Umayyad ambitions and laying the groundwork for Husayn's movement against Yazid's rule.

Disenchanted and disenfranchised by the two decades of Umayyad rule, the Kufans saw with the death of Muawiya a new hope. This could be the chance for Husayn to lead them to the promised nation, they thought. Husayn was not eager for power, however. Like his brother and his father, he turned away from it. "I am better for you as counsel than I am as chief." Those were the words of his father, Ali, when the people came to him to rule after the assassination of Uthman. Though he would eventually lead as caliph, he made it clear to them his purpose and objective: to establish truth and oppose falsehood. Hasan and Husayn learned from their father the art of leadership and the complexity of people's political ambitions and interests, and how to navigate it all while working on their highest priority – preserving the religion of God and the blood of His Prophet's nation.

Some of Husayn's followers had come to him years before, sent him letters, or sought an audience with him in person. At the death of his brother Hasan, some thought that Husayn would have a different policy, a different approach to Muawiya and the Umayyads. He had told his companions and followers that so long as Muawiya was alive, they were to sheathe their swords and remain patient. For a decade, Husayn lived under Muawiya's rule. With Yazid, the circumstances did change. There were certain things about Yazid that were intolerable, from a position of principle. Hasan and Husayn tolerated Muawiya and entered into an accord with him for the benefit of the people and the faith. At that time, no other option would have yielded better results, given the circumstances. With Yazid, however, acquiescing to his rule would not save the faith or the people. While Muawiya maintained a public façade of piety and regard for the tenets of the faith, Yazid was a drunken miscreant who publicly violated what any Muslim would hold sacred. The people of Iraq saw this. They beseeched Husayn once again.

Letters from Kufa came in the thousands to Husayn while he was residing in Mecca. The leaders of Kufa had come together to meet about the future of the nation, and particularly of their communities in Iraq, at the death of Muawiya. They held a conference of sorts, where they took turns giving speeches decrying the crimes of the Umayyads and exclaiming their love and loyalty to Husayn and his family. They expressed their desire for Husayn to come to Iraq, to save them. They said that they would follow him in whatever he asked and would go with him wherever he would go.

Sulaiman al-Khuzai took his turn in speaking to the conveners. He made his position simple and clear:

Muawiya is dead. Husayn had gone out to Mecca after refusing to give allegiance himself. You are his followers and the followers of his father. If you know that you can

> *help him and confront his enemies, then write to him. If*
> *you are fearful of defeat and are apathetic to his cause,*
> *then do not deceive him.*

Sulaiman's short sermon elicited an excited reaction from those present. One man cried out, "I will give my life for him!" Then the rest of them joined him. "We will give our lives for him." They continued to repeat that chant until they came away with a resolution on the way forward for Kufa.

They agreed that Kufa would not succumb to pay allegiance to Yazid and they would send letters to Husayn urging him to move to Kufa and lead them in their cause for just leadership.

One of the most notable letters came from Sulaiman, Habib ibn Muthahir, and a number of other notable loyalists of the Imam. They wrote the following to him:

> *To our Master Husayn,*
>
> *We praise the Almighty and give thanks to Him at the death of your cruelest enemy, Muawiya. He usurped power, stole control of this community, plundered their wealth, and became their ruler without their agreement. He killed the virtuous men of this nation and let the wicked be. He gave the wealth of God to oppressors and opulent people. Then he went away like the Thamud were turned back.*
>
> *There is no leader for us here, so please come and lead us. Perhaps God will keep us on the right path through you. Numan ibn Bashir resides in the governor's palace.*

We do not follow the man or pray behind him on Fridays or the days of Eid. If we know that you are coming to lead us, we will expel him so that he goes back to Syria, if God wills.

May the peace of God be upon you with His endless blessings and bounties

Other letters were shorter, copied and shared in their hundreds, if not thousands. The following was one of those letters:

To Husayn ibn Ali from his followers and Muslims,

Come to us and make haste in it, as people are waiting for you and they do not want anyone else.

So please hurry. Hurry towards us.

And peace be upon you.

There were opportunists who also sent letters, individuals who had no loyalty or love for Husayn or his family. The likes of Shabath ibn Rabai, Hjaar ibn Abjar, and Yazid ibn Harith wrote letters to Husayn. These men would raise their swords against the very men they called on to save them.

The fruits have ripened. The pastures have greened. The rivers have swollen. The time has come and you will find armies mustered at your command. So, come forth. And peace be upon you.

From all different walks of life and varying motivations, Husayn received letters. Though the individuals sending the letters may have differed, one theme was unequivocally the same – come to Iraq. While he was in Mecca, Husayn received letters from messengers daily. It is said that the riders came with saddle bags filled with letters. Husayn received over twelve thousand letters with nearly 140,000 names signing on memorializing their support from the Kufan community. Many of those letters explicitly promised Husayn that there was an army of 100,000 men ready to mobilize for Husayn at a moment's notice. The people wanted Husayn, but for different reasons.

Husayn was aware of the possibilities and the risks that lay ahead. He lived through the bitter betrayals and treachery experienced by his brother and father. Some of that was expected. Out of prudence, the Imam decided to reply to the letters by sending an ambassador to Kufa to assess the situation. He chose his dear cousin and loyal confidant, Muslim ibn Aqeel.

Husayn wrote to the people of Kufa and sent his letter with his ambassador. He made his purpose plain and clear. His appointment of his cousin Muslim was official. Leadership in his eyes was not a matter of vainglory, whim or ambition, it was a matter of God.

> *In the name of God, the Beneficent, the Merciful, From Husayn ibn Ali to all Muslims and believers:*
>
> *Hani and Saeed have arrived before me with your latest letters. They are the last of your messengers who have come to me. They spoke to me just as you wrote to me in your letters. You said:*
>
> *'There is no leader for us here, so please come and lead us. Perhaps God will keep us on the right path through you.'*

Thus, I have sent my brother, the son of my uncle and a reliable member of my family to you. I have instructed him to write to me about your circumstances and to report to me your views about me. If he writes that the views of your elders and the intellectuals amongst you are the same as what your messengers have conveyed and what I have read in your letters, then God willing, I shall set out to meet you at the earliest.

By God, a leader is only one who acts on the Book of God, practices justice, and follows the truth. It is he who has connected himself to the decree of God.

Peace be with you.

Before Muslim left Mecca, Husayn reminded his cousin of his mission. He told Muslim to trust in God and rely on Him alone. He told him to observe piety and watch himself in all that he did. He told Muslim to remember that everything could only be for one purpose. It was all for God. Muslim nodded with confidence, kissed the Imam's hand, and began his journey. They stopped in the city of Medina and paid respects to the tomb of the Prophet before embarking on the journey to Kufa. Muslim's small caravan moved quickly, escaping any spies that tried to follow them. They arrived in Kufa safely.

With the arrival of Muslim in Kufa, there was a huge celebration prepared to welcome him as the ambassador of Husayn. It is said that 18,000 men had gathered in the public square to welcome Muslim and his caravan. They waited for Muslim to speak and deliver the message that came with him from Husayn. Thus,

Muslim read Husayn's letter to them aloud. They wept as they heard their Imam through Muslim's voice.

One after another, people shouted slogans of heartfelt longing and loyalty to Husayn and his family. They said they would give their life for him. They were tired of injustice. They wished to be free. They said that he was their leader, and he would bring them into God's promise of salvation. The people chanted Husayn's name.

Muslim looked upon the thousands that gathered and rejoiced. He was reminded of Husayn's advice to him. Thus, he told the people that in the spirit of the Imam, they must remember to fear God and be weary of those who desired evil and treachery for their community. They promised to be mindful of that and of all that Husayn commanded. With that, they gave their oath of allegiance. Muslim stood at the forefront of the masses that had gathered; alongside him were some of Husayn's eminent companions like Habib ibn Muthahir and Aabis al-Shakiri.

Aabis took a step forward and publicly declared his allegiance and loyalty to Husayn before his ambassador, Muslim. He shared his intentions and expressed his state of mind.

> I stand before you, pledging my allegiance. I cannot warn you about the people, nor can I tell you what is truly in their hearts. I will not deceive you by them. But by God, I will come running to you with your every call. I will fight your enemies alongside you and I will swing my sword for you. I will thrust my spear, defending you

until my very last breath. I will give my life for you. I will fight for you until I meet my Lord, for I do not want anything but that which is with God.

The people that heard Aabis were awe inspired. They were ready to fight and give their life with him. The one it hit home with the most was the man who stood next to him, Habib ibn Muthahir. Habib turned to Aabis and embraced him.

"God bless you for speaking such words. I am of the same view as you. There is no god but Him. We will give our lives in His way," Habib said.

The two brave men nodded at each other and smiled. They had a brotherhood in that love and loyalty for Husayn. That could not be broken. Though the same could not be said for most that stood in the public square of Kufa that day, fate would have it that these two men would live out their promise alongside their master, Husayn.

After such a momentous welcome by an unmatched group of loyalists, Muslim was confident that Husayn would have in this group what he needed of supporters. He quickly wrote a letter to Husayn, describing what he had witnessed, and urged him to make his move to Kufa.

Master Husayn… The people do not lie. 18,000 men of Kufa have given their oath of allegiance to you before me. When you receive this letter, come forward, as all the people are waiting for you. They have no regard nor affinity to Muawiya's clan.

Muslim entrusted Aabis to deliver this letter to Husayn.

"Make haste," He told Aabis. "Have our master come to Kufa at once," Muslim said eagerly.

Muslim had no reason to suspect anything but loyalty and firm resolve from the people of Kufa, after what he witnessed at his arrival. Things would not be so simple. Aabis would reach Husayn in Mecca days later. He delivered the message. The people of Kufa awaited their Imam.

It was then, welcoming the message that came with Aabis, that Husayn announced his decision to move to Kufa.

CHAPTER 8

KUFA HAS A NEW GOVERNOR

Do not try me as your opponent or rival; you will not fare well. I am the son of Ziyad. See me as the man who walks the desert unmoved by its hot days or cold nights. I promise, you will not find in me the compassion of a loving uncle.

– Ubaydallah ibn Ziyad

The governor of Kufa, Numan ibn Bashir, did not forcefully oppose the people that had gathered to welcome Muslim ibn Aqeel en masse. He did not mobilize his police force to crack down on their assembly. He did not infiltrate their ranks. He did not agitate them. He simply let them be. That, of course, did not come without a cost. Numan was ridiculed and criticized for his passiveness by other Umayyad officials in the city. They told him that he was weak and that he could not simply allow the people of Kufa in such a way to do whatever they wanted.

Numan was of a different opinion, one that exhibited a rare piousness of sorts that was uncommon to Umayyad discourse. He explained himself to one of his colleagues, Abdullah al-Hadhrami, who questioned him.

Numan firmly proclaimed, "I shall not employ any method that distances us from God and I will not step towards any path that takes me away from religion." Abdullah was puzzled.

In short, Abdullah and the rest of the Umayyad agents in Kufa knew that Numan was not the man for the job anymore. Abdullah wrote immediately to Damascus and informed them of the dire need for action regarding the governor. Revolution was fast approaching and the local government in Kufa was not going to do anything about it with Numan in the governor's palace. He wrote:

> *You must know that Muslim ibn Aqeel has come to Kufa. The people have pledged allegiance through him for Husayn ibn Ali. If you desire to keep Kufa under your control, then send a strongman to govern it immediately. That way you can impose your command and deal with the enemies the way you would like. Numan ibn Bashir is a weak man or at the very least, he chooses to be weak.*

Other loyalists to the Umayyads wrote similar letters to Yazid, such as Ammara ibn Walid ibn Uqbah as well as Umar ibn Saad. The message was received loud and clear. Yazid could not sleep until he deposed Numan and replaced him with a strongman that would quell the revolution that was well on its way. He lay awake at night thinking about Iraq. His father had crushed them under his rule. When Muawiya was caliph in the years prior, he entered Kufa and made a clear declaration to its people.

"I have not come to promote prayer and pilgrimage, I have come to rule over you and this treaty I signed with Hasan ibn Ali is under my foot," proclaimed Muawiya.

Yazid knew how heavy-handed his father was. He loved it. But now he had to deal with the consequences of an angered people who were filled with hope at the sight of their champion coming to save them.

Yazid was still in the first months of his rulership. He did not know what to do or how to solve this predicament of Kufa. He turned to a man named Sarjun, who had been one of the most senior advisors to his father Muawiya. Sarjun was a Christian political strategist of sorts with a wealth of experience across the Byzantine and Arabian lands. Muawiya advised Yazid, before he passed, to keep Sarjun in his close circle and benefit from him just as he had. He told him that Sarjun would give him insights that are often overlooked. He was good to have around. So Yazid complied. Sarjun would stay close.

Yazid paced back and forth on the balcony of his chambers. Sarjun stood nearby.

"What am I to do, Sarjun? Husayn is making his way to Kufa and his ambassador has already accepted people's allegiance. And my governor in Kufa is a weak imbecile!"

"Would you like your father's opinion in the matter?" Sarjun replied to Yazid as he looked at the horizon from the terrace.

"My father?" Yazid replied intrigued.

"Your father left this order before he died," Sarjun said as he handed Yazid a letter with Muawiya's seal. "If he were here now, he would have Ubaydallah ibn Ziyad take hold of Kufa and its people."

Yazid despised the man. Ubaydallah was the governor of Basra. He succeeded his father, Ziyad, after he passed away in 673 AD. Ziyad had been grooming his son for the position. Ziyad was seen as an effective military commander and governor, one who was eager to expand dominion for the empire. Muawiya appointed him as the governor of Basra in 665 AD. There was an interesting personal relationship between Ziyad and Muawiya.

Ziyad's parentage was obscure. It was not said with certainty who his parents were. He was often referred to as Ziyad ibn Abihi (the son of his father), given that his paternity was not known for sure. When Muawiya came to power, Ziyad did not refrain from showing him opposition. Muawiya would embrace Ziyad and officially recognize him as his half-brother and the son of his own father, Abu Sufyan. This created an uproar within the ruling Umayyad family and the decision was especially despised by Muawiya's heir apparent, Yazid. Muawiya's decision to recognize Ziyad as Ziyad ibn Abi Sufyan automatically gave Ziyad's own sons, especially the most ambitious amongst them, Ubaydallah, a broader sense of entitlement within the Umayyad regime.

Ubaydallah opposed Yazid's coming to power and refused to pay allegiance to him when Muawiya was alive. For that, Yazid had been planning to have him deposed as a punishment for Ibn Ziyad's insubordination. The reality was that if any governor in the Umayyad regime could quell a rebellion and suppress a group thinking of mutiny, it was Ubaydallah ibn Ziyad. Ubaydallah was a ruthless dictator. He had no regard for human life. Nothing was sacred to him. Power was his only aim and sub-jugation was his method. Yazid realized this and he trusted Sar-jun's advice. Not only was Ibn Ziyad kept in his post, but Yazid decided to make him the governor of Kufa as well. The designa-tion essentially made him the governor of all of Iraq. Yazid sent explicit instructions to Ibn Ziyad.

> Our agents in Kufa report to us that Muslim ibn Aqeel is rallying people in Kufa for purposes of sedition and mutiny. When you receive this letter, you are to leave for Kufa immediately. Do not rest until you get a hold of Muslim. It is your choice to throw him in prison or have his head.

Ibn Ziyad received Yazid's letter as he sat on his throne. He was ecstatic. He began salivating at the thought of crushing the rebels of Kufa. It was said that he took pleasure in torturing peo-ple. So, he did as he was instructed by the caliph, who he now would call the Commander of the Faithful Yazid. Before he left Basra to march on to Kufa, he gathered the people of Basra and delivered a short speech:

> The Commander of the Faithful Yazid has appointed me as the governor of Kufa. I shall leave for Kufa tomor-row. By Allah, I shall not refrain from using force and no evil shall stop me. Whoever becomes hostile to me shall be destroyed by me. Because I am a poison to eve-ryone who makes war on me.

O people of Basra, I appoint my brother Uthman ibn Ziyad ibn Abi Sufyan as my viceroy over you. Never disobey or disregard his orders. By God, if I hear of any one of you opposing him in any way, you will be eliminated – you, your men, and your supporters.

Do not try me as your opponent or rival; you will not fare well. I am the son of Ziyad. See me as the man who walks the desert unmoved by its hot days or cold nights. I promise, you will not find in me the compassion of a loving uncle.

The people of Basra did not need to take his word for it, they witnessed his force before, and they were not about to test him again. Ibn Ziyad marched on to Kufa.

The journey was a harsh one. Ibn Ziyad had left with hundreds of men. But they did not travel as fast as he liked. He was thirsty to arrive in Kufa. Instead of waiting for his men to catch up, he rode on until he arrived to the city on his own. Before entering the city, Ibn Ziyad disguised himself with a black turban and simple clothing. He covered his face with a dark veil. His intention was to fool people into thinking that he was Husayn ibn Ali.

It actually worked. The people that saw him ride into town cheered him on, thinking it was Husayn. He went directly to the governor's palace. The doors were locked. Numan stood at the balcony above watching him.

"Open the doors!" Ibn Ziyad called out.

"I invoke God before you! Leave me be! By God, I will not hand over my office to you, but I have no wish to fight you either!"

Numan thought he was speaking to Husayn. Ibn Ziyad could tell the old man was weak. He did not have the patience for it.

"Open now! You have not opened yet and you have already had a long night." Ibn Ziyad insinuated that Numan was sleeping when he should have been governing.

People had gathered behind Ibn Ziyad thinking he was Husayn. When they heard him speak, they realized it was not Husayn after all. Shocked and perturbed, the group that had gathered ran away and dispersed. Soon enough, Ibn Ziyad gathered the Umayyad agents, deposed of Numan, and took control of the police force and the treasury.

The morning came and Ibn Ziyad ordered that people be gathered. He led congregational prayers and gave a speech. He carried a message from the Caliph.

The Commander of the faithful Yazid has appointed me in charge of your town, your frontier-station, and the distribution of your treasury. He has ordered me to give justice to the oppressed among you, to be generous to those of you who are deprived, and to treat the obedient among you with generosity like a good father, but to use the whip and the sword against those who abandon my commands and oppose my appointment. Let each man protect himself. True belief should declare itself on your behalf, not the threat of punishment.

Though he made no mention of Husayn or his ambassador, Muslim, the message was clear. That morning, Ibn Ziyad mobilized his police force to make hundreds of arrests. They targeted the homes of those who were known loyalists to Husayn. Muslim quickly changed where he had been staying to avert the threat of being captured by Ibn Ziyad's men. It is said that Muslim left Mukhtar al-Thaqafi's house and moved to stay with Hani ibn Urwa. Mukhtar was soon arrested and thrown in prison with the hundreds of others.

Hani was a unique character and a strategic partner. He was widely respected and had a huge following from his tribe. He had the affluence and influence to protect Muslim. Hani welcomed Muslim into his home with open arms, knowing the possible danger ahead. He would not refuse him, both out of respect for tradition to never turn away a guest and in observance of the principle of supporting the people of truth.

Hani's home was open to many. It is said that man by the name of Shareek ibn Aawar had been staying with Hani and he had fallen ill. In Ibn Ziyad's effort to connect with the nobles of Kufa and embrace those with influence, he decided to visit Shareek and wish him well.

Shareek was an ally of Muslim. He told Muslim and Hani that Ibn Ziyad's visit was the perfect opportunity to kill the new governor while he least expected it. He turned to Muslim and told him what he thought Muslim should do.

"Ibn Ziyad is on his way here. Go and hide in the closet. When he sits with me, relaxed, jump out and slay him with your sword. Then you can go to the palace and be in full command of the city. No one will oppose you. And I promise you, if God gives me my health, I will go to Basra and do the same for you. The people there will give you their allegiance as well. Take my word.

Hani shook his head and said in a low voice, "I do not like the idea of him being killed in my home."

Shareek shrugged off Hani's concern and told Muslim that he had to take this opportunity and be done with the tyrant once and for all. Soon enough, Ibn Ziyad was at their doorstep. Muslim quickly hid in the nearest closet.

Ibn Ziyad sat beside Shareek and Hani.

"How are you doing, brother?" Ibn Ziyad said as he touched Shareek's bedside.

Shareek moaned and groaned about his condition. He spoke of his ailments, stalling for Muslim to come out and seize the moment to take Ibn Ziyad's life and be rid of the tyrant once and for all. But Muslim remained hidden.

Shareek tried to make his signal more apparent in reciting a verse of poetry:

For whom do you await,

That you do not welcome Salmi?

Welcome him and whosoever welcomes him,

Give the goblet of death!

Still, no Muslim. Shareek was getting nervous. He did not want this chance to slip away. He raised his voice and called out.

May God give reward you and your father!

Give him the drink even if my life is lost in its drips.

Ibn Ziyad leaned back in his chair with his arms crossed and eyebrows raised. He turned to Hani and asked, "Is the man delirious?"

"Yes, governor. He's been like this since the morning," Hani nervously explained.

Ibn Ziyad's assistant, Mihran, was suspicious of them. He did not buy it. He gestured to Ibn Ziyad and got up hastily, so as to attend to other urgent business. Ibn Ziyad understood something was up.

"Governor, but I wish to speak to you some more," Shareek pleaded as Ibn Ziyad was getting up to leave.

"Sure, I will visit you again soon." Ibn Ziyad said on his way out.

As they walked away from the house, Ibn Ziyad asked Mihran, "What is it, Mihran? What happened?"

Mihran turned to the governor and said, "They wanted to kill you, master. I could feel it."

"After all the respect I gave to him and in the house of Hani out of all places?! My father liked the man," Ibn Ziyad was troubled. "I will show them." They proceeded to the governor's palace.

Back at the house, Muslim opened the door of the closet and came out to sit with Hani and Shareek again. They were all sweating. Shareek was very upset.

"Why didn't you come out and kill him? It was your only chance," Shareek said, defeated.

Muslim nodded. "For one, Hani did not want the man killed in his house. I could not ignore that. Two, the Prophet of God said that a believer never takes a life by way of deceit. This was simply not the way for us."

Shareek died days later. Ibn Ziyad was onto Hani and Muslim. It was only a matter of time.

Hani was eventually summoned to the governor's palace. He reluctantly complied, escorted by some of Ibn Ziyad's men. Interrogated about his loyalty to Muslim and his harboring of the man in his home, an argument ensued between Hani and Ibn Ziyad. After Hani denied Muslim's presence in his home, Ibn Ziyad presented the spy he planted amongst them, so Hani finally stated that he would never give up Muslim.

"I will not betray Muslim! I will not hand him over!"

"You are to bring him to me or I will have your head," Ibn Ziyad threatened.

"Then you will see the flashing of our swords," Hani promised.

Ibn Ziyad lowered his voice and took a deep breath. "Hani, come near me." Hani hesitated. "Come closer, old friend."

Hani took a few steps closer to Ibn Ziyad. At that moment, the governor swung his cane and struck Hani in the face. He swung at him again and again. Ibn Ziyad broke his nose and blood was gushing from Hani's forehead. Ibn Ziyad had struck Hani so many times with the cane that it eventually broke. Hani's gray beard was stained with his own crimson red blood.

Hani tried to grab at one of the guard's swords to defend himself, but he was not successful.

"Take this imbecile away!" the governor shouted. Hani was dragged out of the hall and thrown into a small room and locked away.

One of the men, Hisan ibn Asma, was in disbelief. He looked at Ibn Ziyad and protested, "Are we agents of treachery now? You told us to bring the man to you so that you may speak to him. We did as you asked but you smashed the man's nose in, pummeled his face, and bloodied his beard! Now you want to have him killed!"

"Yes, and you will be witness to it here and now," Ibn Ziyad replied. "Take care of him." The governor had Hisan beaten and thrown to the side.

Hani would be executed. He was made an example of. Even one of the most influential men in Kufan community, with thousands of tribesman, would be killed. Ibn Ziyad's political manipulation, trickery, mass roundups, and swift executions would prove to outmaneuver what Muslim had garnered in support. The force that Muslim had built, with the help of his uncle Ali's companions like Habib ibn Muthahir and Muslim ibn Awsaja, had dwindled over the days that followed. People feared for their lives, the families, and their livelihoods. Ibn Ziyad took advantage of those fears and capitalized on them. He fooled those that could be fooled, scared those that could be scared, imprisoned and even killed those that could not be contained.

Muslim moved from house to house to evade Ibn Ziyad's police force that was searching for him day and night. But soon enough, no place was safe anymore for Husayn's ambassador.

Muslim would find himself one night at the doorstep of a pious woman, named Tawaa, who would reluctantly give him shelter. Her son was not so pious. Eager to gain a reward from the governor, he sold out Muslim's hiding place at the break of dawn. The young man filled his pockets with gold and silver, while Muslim was surrounded by hundreds of Ibn Ziyad's troops. Muslim did not surrender. He fought valiantly and refused to put down his sword until he could lift his sword no longer. They dragged Muslim, who had been bloodied from head to toe with battle wounds across his body from the arrest, into the governor's palace, where Ibn Ziyad would await.

It was not long before Ibn Ziyad ordered his execution from the roof top of the palace. At the execution, Muslim was asked for any last wishes. He made three requests. The first was to pay a small debt by selling his sword and armor, the second was to give his body a proper burial, and the third was to deliver a message to his beloved Husayn. That was what weighed heaviest on Muslim's heart, that Husayn was coming forth to this place.

"Tell Husayn not to come to Kufa, for it is not as it seemed to be," Muslim cried.

Ibn Ziyad half-heartedly agreed to the first request and rejected the other two without hesitation. Muslim was beheaded mercilessly and his body was thrown from the rooftop of the palace. Ibn Ziyad did not bat an eye.

The corpses of both Hani and Muslim were tied to horseback and dragged through the streets of Kufa. Their bodies were hoisted at the gates of the city as a warning to all near and far. This was the fate of those who opposed the Umayyads. Yazid received their heads as a gift from his coldblooded governor, Ubaydallah ibn Ziyad.

While many of Husayn's supporters in Kufa were imprisoned or killed, a handful of them, like Habib ibn Muthahir and Muslim ibn Awsaja, managed to escape and join the caravan of Husayn as they journeyed towards their final destination.

CHAPTER 9

THE ROAD TO IRAQ

Anyone who joins me shall be martyred and one who does not join me shall not obtain success.

– Husayn ibn Ali

Husayn would leave Mecca to protect the sanctuary that was the Kaaba, as the Umayyads had expressed that they would kill Husayn even if he were holding on to the cloth that covered God's House. Though Husayn was not afraid of death, he knew that dying then and there would not fulfill his purpose and mission. Muslim's letter, coupled with Husayn's desire to protect the sanctity of the Kaaba, made the move to Iraq the best decision for him given all the circumstances.

Before Husayn's departure from Mecca, he sent a letter to his relatives from the tribe of Hashim.

> *From Husayn ibn Ali to his brother, Muhammad, and anyone who is with him from Banu Hashim:*
>
> *Anyone who joins me shall be martyred and one who does not join me shall not obtain success, and peace be upon you all.*

He proceeded to give his final sermon at the Kaaba before finally leaving the sanctuary of God. The people had gathered before him. He began in God's name, just as he always had.

Praise is to God. By God's will, and there is no power save but with God, peace and blessings upon His Messenger and his family.

Death is bound with the sons of Adam as a necklace around the neck of a maiden. How I desire and long to meet my ancestors, just like Jacob who wished to see his son, Joseph. I proceed towards the place of my martyrdom, which has been selected for me. It is as if I see the wolves of the desert separating each part of my body between Nawawis and Karbala. With it they fill their empty bellies. There is no escape from that which has been written down by the pen of destiny.

The contentment of our household lies in the pleasure of God alone. Verily we will endure His trials and secure the reward due to the patient. The connection between the Prophet and his son will never break. Instead, we will all be united with him near God in Heaven. The Prophet's eyes will be cooled with our presence and God will fulfill what He has promised.

Whoever wishes to lay down his life for us and strive in the way of God should come with us. I will be leaving tomorrow morning, God willing.

Sadly, though a huge crowd was present, listening to the Imam deliver this final sermon of his in Mecca, only a few believers actually joined him. Heedlessness was at an all-time high. The people were in a deep spiritual slumber. Salvation was right in front of them, the beaming sun of deliverance was shining in all its glory, but they could not even see it.

Husayn's journey to Iraq took place over about two weeks and involved a number of stops along the way. Naturally, these stops gave his family some time to rest after each day's tiring journey across the hot deserts of Arabia. There were also significant meetings, speeches, and revelations that took place on these stops and along the way.

The Imam's first stop came at a town called Saffah. There he was met by a renowned poet named Farazdaq. As the poet sat with Husayn for a while, Husayn asked him about his impressions of the people of Kufa. Farazdaq paused for a moment. He looked off into the desert, as if searching in the desert winds for the words to describe what Kufa would be for Husayn. He then found the right expression:

Their hearts are with you, but their swords are against you.

Farazdaq famously said those words and they are forever remembered for his foresight. Husayn's reply would be equally telling:

God does what He wishes. I leave it all to Him.

Husayn's absolute reliance on God was unmatched. His mission was clear. With all the warnings in the world of the betrayal that could come from the people of Kufa, and all people for that matter, Husayn was unrelenting in his faith and conviction in God.

As Husayn and his family continued on their journey, they were met with some family members that caught up to them not too far from Mecca. It was in Dhat el-Irq that Husayn's brother-in-law, Abdullah ibn Jafar, Lady Zaynab's husband, met them. Abdullah brought his sons Aoun and Muhammad to join their mother, Zaynab, and support their uncle Husayn on their journey. Abdullah tried again to persuade Husayn to come back to Medina and reconsider his move to Iraq. Husayn gave a simple reply to his cousin:

My destiny is with God.

When Husayn stopped in place called Batn el-Rumma, he wrote a letter to send to his cousin Muslim in Kufa. He wished to let him know of his progress on the journey and to ask for further developments in Kufa. The messenger that was returning to Iraq, and whom Husayn wished to send his letter with, tried convincing the Imam to reconsider his journey to Kufa. Husayn again refused and reiterated his conviction.

Husayn then made a stop in town called Dhurud. There his family and friends spent some time to rest and regroup. In each town that Husayn stopped in up until this point, more and more people joined his caravan. Husayn's charisma and purity made people gravitate towards him. There were those who also saw his movement as an opportunity for material gain. Some did not fare so well with the Umayyads. They were disenfranchised and marginalized. Others were simply not given the extra benefits that their neighbors may have received. Husayn's opposition to Yazid was seen by some of these groups as a chance to get ahead, to take part in the spoils of battle, or possibly be appointed a position in a new government.

Husayn would have none of that. Though his doors were wide open to all, he did not campaign or rally people around him. He was forthright and honest. He repeated his intentions and made clear what his journey was all about. "Reformation in the nation of my grandfather." His purpose was clear. "Whoever joins us will be martyred and the ones who do not join me will not see success", he promised. While this discouraged many, when Zuhayr ibn al-Qayn heard the Imam while he was in Zurud, he pledged allegiance to him. Zuhayr was not a loyalist or a follower of Ali. But when he heard Husayn speak with such sincerity and conviction, he was resolute on joining him and giving him his life. It is said that Zuhayr went to his wife and gave her everything that he owned, except his sword and shield.

Puzzled by his frantic movements, his wife asked him, "Where are you going, Zuhayr?"

"You own everything that is mine now. I am going with Husayn ibn Ali," he replied.

"Well, where is he going?" she exclaimed.

"To be martyred."

Zuhayr joined Husayn's caravan and they continued their journey towards their destiny. The farther they traveled, the more apparent their fate became. At this point, hundreds of

other men, some say even thousands, had joined Husayn's caravan to Iraq. When they reached the town of Zabala, Husayn received the terrible news from Kufa. Muslim was captured, tortured, and executed by Ibn Ziyad.

We are for God and to Him we shall return.

Husayn continued to repeat those words as his eyes watered
over his cousin, Muslim. The men gathered around him to learn
of what had transpired. Husayn did not hide the news from
them. He wanted them to know what they would be taking part
in. He wanted them to know that this soon could be their fate
too if they stayed by his side. He stood before them and let them
know loud and clear:

> *I have received tragic news. Muslim ibn Aqeel, Hani ibn
> Urwa, and Abdullah ibn Yaqtur were all murdered. We
> have been abandoned by our followers. Whoever of you
> wishes to leave now will not be blamed.*

Husayn walked away, giving people a chance to make their
decision to leave or remain without being pressured. Husayn ab-
horred the idea that people would follow his caravan for the
wrong reasons, that they were embarking on a journey they do
not understand. Some joined because they thought Husayn
would certainly come to rule. That was not his plan nor his fate.
He wanted them to know where he was headed. Even when some
in the group tried to persuade him to reconsider carrying on
with the journey, especially with the news of Muslim's death,
Husayn respectfully refused.

Though you may be sound in what you say, God's will cannot be undone.

Walking back to the women and children, Husayn found that the majority of the men who had joined the caravan had left. Only about fifty remained. He was pleased. People made their choice. Their lives were sacred to him. His sacrifice was his own. That was for him to bear and carry. If their lives could be spared, he would have it. Thus, throughout his journey, Husayn gave those who joined him one opportunity after another to leave him, without blame. Those who remained were a rare breed. They saw sacrifice with Husayn as their calling, their honor, and their life's work before their Lord.

Town after town, Husayn was met with warnings about Kufa. At a place called Batn el-Ateeq, he was told that Ibn Ziyad had closed off Kufa. No one was allowed to enter, and no one was allowed to leave. They said that he executed hundreds and imprisoned thousands. Husayn did not stray from his path forward. It was not about arriving in Kufa, for him. It was fulfilling his destiny and taking this journey on the path of God. His hope remained in God. He would show him the way.

When they arrived near the town of Dhuhasm, Husayn's caravan spotted an army approaching. It was Hur ibn Yazid al-Riyahi with one thousand men sent by Ubaydallah ibn Ziyad. Hur's orders were stop Husayn from reaching Kufa unless he paid allegiance to Yazid ibn Muawiya. Otherwise, he was to be apprehended and brought forth to the governor.

The day before Hur's battalion had arrived, Husayn had ordered his sons to gather water for their caravan. When the soldiers came forth, Husayn saw how thirsty they were. He called them forth and invited them to drink.

"Give the men water and let them quench their thirst. Give their horses water to drink as well," Husayn told his sons.

He even gave them water by his own hand, quenching the thirst of Hur's men. Hur watched in awe, as the man that he was tasked to arrest treated his men with the greatest compassion and kindness.

The time of midday prayer came. Husayn told one of his men to make the adhan, the call to prayer. *Allahu Akbar!* God is great. His voice echoed in the name of God under the open desert sky. Husayn turned to Hur and his men.

> *I did not come here to you until your letters came to me, and they were brought by your messengers. 'Come to us, for we have no Imam. Through you, may God unite us under guidance and truth,' the letters wrote. Since this was your view, I have come to you. Therefore, give me what you guaranteed in your covenants and testimonies. If you will not and if now you are against me coming forth, then I will leave and go back to where I came from.*

None of them uttered a word. Husayn was met with silence. The men stood their ground and did not move. Husayn understood, they were not changing course. He nodded and looked at Hur. He asked him if Hur wanted to lead his men in prayer.

"You can pray, and we will follow," Hur replied.

Husayn led prayers and all those present followed. After the prayers, Husayn turned again to Hur and his men and repeated similar words he mentioned before prayer. He reminded them that he was the grandson of the Holy Prophet and that he had only come forward at the request of the people. He emphasized the many letters and messengers that had come to him from Iraq.

"I know nothing of these letters and messengers," replied Hur.

Husayn gestured to one of his men to grab something from his tent. The man came forward moments later with two large saddle-bags filled with thousands of letters. He placed them before Hur. Hur looked down at the bags and back up at Husayn.

"We did not write these letters to you, Husayn. Our orders are to escort you to the governor of Kufa."

"Death will come to you before that is to happen," Husayn responded in short. He gestured for his followers to get mounted on their horses. They ascended on their mounts, the women and children as well, and began to move.

Hur's men stopped them and prevented them from moving forward. Husayn faced off with Hur, who stood between him and the road to Kufa. Hur was adamant on fulfilling the orders he came with. He would not let Husayn go forward.

Husayn looked at Hur and said, "May your mother be deprived of you!"

"If any other Arab were to say this to me, my response would be in kind. But I could not say such a thing to you when your mother is Fatima," Hur humbly replied.

"What do you want?" Husayn demanded.

"I wish to escort you to the governor."

"I will not follow you."

"Then I cannot let you go anywhere else."

Both men would not budge. Hur was following strict orders. Husayn had a higher calling. Hur explained himself.

"I have not been ordered to fight you. My orders are to escort you to Kufa. If you do not comply, you will not be allowed to continue on to Kufa or go back to Medina. That is the compromise until I write to the governor."

Seeing no other way, Husayn began to take another road – one that does not go to Kufa nor back to Medina, as Hur suggested. Hur and his men followed close by.

"Husayn, I remind you to think of your life. You will be killed if you fight," Hur warned.

Husayn stopped his horse and faced Hur again. "Do you think you frighten me with death? If I live, I will not regret this. If I die, I will not suffer. It should be enough for you to realize that you will live disgraced and detested."

Husayn's words deeply affected Hur. His silence was enough to show that. Hur and his men continued to travel close by to Husayn's caravan, riding on the other side of the road.

Husayn's caravan continued to ride to the town ahead. Ali al-Akbar, Husayn's eldest son, was riding his horse beside his father. He noticed his father was tired. He also noticed that he kept repeating the holy verse:

We belong to God and to Him we will return.

After a few times of hearing him repeat the verse, Ali turned to his father and asked him plainly, "Father, why do you keep repeating the verse of returning to God?"

Husayn replied, "I nodded off and a horseman appeared to me. He said, 'Men are travelling and the fates travel towards them.' Then I knew it was our own souls proclaiming our deaths to us."

Ali nodded and asked, "Father, are we not on the path of truth?"

"Indeed, we are my son," Husayn replied, "by Him to whom all His servants must return."

Ali smiled. "Then we have no worries, as we will die on this path of truth."

Husayn smiled back. "May God give you the best reward my son, for you have honored your father."

It was a proud moment for Husayn, seeing the conviction in his son's heart. Even more than pride and joy, Husayn had with his son a heart at ease – a calm in knowing that no matter what would lie ahead, his sons would own up to the challenge and manifest for themselves the greatest reward with God. For their sacrifice for God and His religion was matched by none.

The morning came and along with it, news from Kufa. After morning prayer, Husayn and Hur watched the messenger ride so fast towards them. He jumped off his horse and greeted Hur, ignoring Husayn. The messenger handed him a letter of instruction from Ubaydallah ibn Ziyad. Hur opened the sealed letter and silently read to himself.

> *When this letter reaches you with my messenger, make Husayn come to a halt. Only let him stop in an open place without vegetation. My messenger has strict orders from me not to leave you, until you have carried out my instructions.*

Hur looked at the messenger from the corner of his eye. He was watching Hur. His task was clear. Do no leave until Hur besieges Husayn under the open sky where there is no town or vegetation to give him drink or shade. Hur carried out the orders. As his men began pushing Husayn's caravan to such a place, Husayn protested.

"Shame on you, let us stop at one of these villages," Husayn said to Hur.

Hur came closer to Husayn and replied in a low voice, "By God, I cannot. This man is here only to see that this is done."

As Hur rode off to lead the rest of his men, Zuhayr came closer to Husayn to share a thought. "I can only think that after what you have seen, the situation will only get worse. Fighting these people, now, will be easier for us than fighting those who will come against us after them. For after them will come against us a number so great that we will not have the power to fight against them."

Looking at the horizon and back at Zuhayr, Husayn made his position clear: "I will not be the one to commence in the fight against them."

The caravan continued moving some more, until something overcame the Imam and he stopped. He asked, "What is the name of this land?"

One of the men replied, "Karbala."

Husayn sighed, "Indeed, this is the land of Karb-wa-bala." The place of *pain and suffering*. "We will stop here. This is our destination. This is where we will be martyred. This is Karbala." It was the second day of the new lunar year, in the holy month of Muharram.

The caravan came to a full stop and their tents were set up. The next day, Umar ibn Saad left Kufa at the command of the governor with four thousand cavalries. They stopped at the nearby land of Ninawa. Before engaging Husayn directly, Umar sent a messenger to ask what Husayn wanted. Husayn reiterated what he said to Hur. If the people did not want him, he would return. He did not want bloodshed, only what was best for the people at their request. The messenger went back to Umar and shared what Husayn said.

"I hope God will spare me from this war and fighting against him," Umar said to himself. He sat down and wrote a letter reporting back to the governor.

I write this from where I am stationed near Husayn's camp. I asked him what brought him and what he wants. He said, 'The people of this land wrote to me and their messengers came to me asking me to come and I have done so. However, if they have changed their minds and now their position is different from what their messengers brought to me, I will leave.'

When Umar's letter came to Ubaydallah, he read it and scoffed. "You see! Now when our claws are around his neck, he hopes for escape! But he will not be given any safety from us. No, he will not."

The governor wrote to his commander plainly.

Your letter has reached me and I have understood what you mentioned. Tell Husayn that he, and all his followers, can pledge allegiance to Yazid. If he does that, we will then see what our judgement will be.

Umar read this letter and looked up shaking his head. "I fear that Ubaydallah will not spare me from this battle as I had wished."

CHAPTER 10

A LETTER OF SECURITY

O sons of my sister! I have guaranteed your security with the noble governor Ubaydallah!

– Shimr ibn Dhil-Jawshan

At the governor's palace, Shimr ibn Thil-Jawshan and Abdullah ibn Abilmuhil were in the presence of Ubaydallah ibn Ziyad. They were cousins. Ibn Abilmuhil was a nephew of Ummul Baneen, the widow of Imam Ali. She had four sons – Abbas, Jafar, Uthman, and Abdullah – all of whom were soldiers in the camp of Husayn.

Before leaving the presence of the governor, Shimr and Ibn Abilmuhil stood up and asked permission to speak.

"May the governor be protected by God's grace," Ibn Abilmuhil said as he bowed before Ibn Ziyad. "Our nephews are along with Husayn. If you deem fit, perhaps give us a letter of security for them."

"Very well," Ubaydallah replied. He ordered his scribe to write the letter guaranteeing Abbas and his brothers safety at once.

Ibn Abilmuhil sent the letter to Karbala with Kurman, his messenger. "Leave Kufa at once, and take this to my nephews," Ibn Abilmuhil instructed Kurman.

"Yes sir," Kurman replied and was on his way.

Upon arriving in Karbala's open desert plains, Kurman spotted the camp of Husayn. A humble setting of tents sat on a sloping hilltop. Kurman made his way over and navigated through the camp, asking for the sons of Ummul Baneen.

"There is the tent of Abbas," one of the guards pointed to him. Kurman was granted permission to enter the tent, where he found Abbas sitting with his brothers.

"Salaamu Alaykum, master Abbas," Kurman said as he placed his hand on his chest.

"Wa Alaykum Asalaam," Abbas replied, looking the man in his eyes.

"I come with word from your uncle, Abdullah ibn Abilmuhil," Kurman stated.

"What does our uncle say?" Abbas asked.

"He has sent this sealed document of security for you and your brothers," Kurman said as he extended the sealed scroll towards Abbas.

Abbas smiled.

"Convey our greetings to our uncle and tell him that we are in no need of his security," Abbas replied, while his hands remained in his lap. "Verily, Allah's security is better than that of the son of Sumayyah." Kurman placed his hand on his chest, slightly bowing his head and retreated from the tent back to Kufa.

The next day, Shimr approached the camp of Husayn with a battalion of soldiers. Seeing them approaching from outside his tent, Abbas came to his brother Husayn and informed him of the troops' presence.

"Master Husayn, Ubaydallah ibn Ziyad's troops have come." Husayn rose from his seat.

"Mount your horse and go to them dear brother. See what it is that they want," Husayn ordered. "And if they are adamant on battle, give us the night for our Lord."

Abbas placed his hand on his heart and obliged. He took a group of warriors with him, including his brothers, Abdullah, Jafar, and Uthman.

As Abbas and his brothers rode towards the caliphate's battalion, Shimr bellowed in the faces of the companions that stood guard.

"Where are the sons of our clan sister?"

Abbas and his brothers came to the forefront from behind the ranks.

"What do you want, Shimr?" Abbas asked plainly.

"O sons of my sister!" Shimr replied, extending his arms. "I have guaranteed your security with the noble governor, Ubaydallah!"

"And what of security for the grandson of God's Messenger?" Abbas asked.

"You and your brothers are safe with us. Our issue is with Husayn. Leave him," Shimr replied.

Abbas responded sharply, "Damn you and your security, Shimr!" Abbas then turned to the rest of the men and said, "Shall we obey the accursed sons and their accursed fathers?"

The small band of companions roared behind Abbas in unison, "No we shall not!"

"Brothers, what say you of Master Husayn?"

"We wait to die for you, O Husayn!" the brothers thundered.

"Like I said to our uncle's messenger," Abbas followed. "Keep your security for those who need it."

Shimr was enraged. He turned red in the face.

"Then you give us no other choice. Any last wishes?" Shimr yelled.

"We know that is what you came for, Shimr. You shall have your battle. But let it be tomorrow."

"Tomorrow?"

"Yes. Husayn's only request is to delay your battle until to-morrow."

"What use will that be?" Shimr inquired.

"Husayn wants one last night in this world to pray to his Lord," Abbas replied.

Shimr chuckled. "His prayers will not help him."

"If only you knew what his prayers can do," Abbas replied.

Abbas and his men turned around and rode away. Shimr shouted at his battalion to return to camp.

CHAPTER 11

THE EVE OF ASHURA

I give you all leave, tonight. I relieve each of you from the oath of allegiance you have pledged to me.

– Husayn ibn Ali

The eve of the tenth day of Muharram, Ashura, had arrived. It was a still night for the camp of Husayn. The Prophet's grandson gathered his companions – men who prepared their souls for the inevitable battle of the morrow. They were outside under the open sky, some pacing back and forth, some sitting around a fire, some praying and supplicating. The crackling of wood, the fire's smoke rising into the starry night, and the glowing red ambers set the scene for Husayn's speech. As Husayn stepped forward from his tent, the men all stood up in unison. Battle formation was just a cue away. The flagbearer, Abbas, was ready. They stood eager for the command of their leader. All stopped. Everything was still.

"I glorify God with the best glorification, and praise him in times of prosperity as well as misfortune," Husayn began. "Dear God, I praise You that You have honored our family with the Holy Prophet. You revealed the Quran to us, so that we understood Your religion. You gave us foresight and an enlightened heart. Bring us into the fold of your grateful servants."

Husayn's companions continued to gaze at him without disruption. Many were not merely warriors, but scholars and mystics in their own right. They were men of God, who savored every remembrance of His highest name.

"I do not know any companions who are more faithful and devout than you," Husayn said as he touched the shoulders of his men. "Nor have I known any family who is more considerate, affectionate, and gracious than my own." Husayn smiled at his brothers and sons. "I pray that God rewards you well on my behalf."

Husayn paused, looking upon the fire and the smoke that would continue to rise above them. "The enemy will not spare another day without commencing this inescapable battle. Tomorrow I will face my death, and anyone who remains with me will have a similar fate," Husayn said solemnly.

Opening his hands and extending his arms, he exclaimed, "I give you all leave, tonight. I relieve each of you from the oath of allegiance you have pledged to me." The men's faces turned stern. The mere thought of abandoning their allegiance to Husayn, with his permission or not, pained them. Husayn continued, "The darkness of the night will protect you. So, ride into the night and take a family member of mine with you. Lay low in a village or city of your choice, until some time has passed. These people want my blood alone, and after they have it, they will not pursue anyone else."

Husayn's brothers, sons and nephews stepped forward as a battalion of their own with Abbas at their forefront. "Master Husayn, this will not happen We have no desire to remain alive after you."

They followed in unison, "Our life is for you!"

Amongst them were Husayn's cousins, the brothers and sons of Muslim ibn Aqeel. Husayn looked at them and remembered his cousin, Muslim, who had fallen at the hands of tyranny in Kufa.

"The sacrifice of Muslim is enough to bear. Please take my permission to free yourselves of any further burden," Husayn said to them with a broken smile.

The brothers looked at one another and shook their heads. "Our brother Muslim did his part. He savored the glory of God. But what of us? Will history say that we had forsaken our leader? That we left our cousin to the wolves? Could it be that the sons of Aqeel will not shoot arrows alongside the sons of Ali, that they will not thrust their spears and strike their swords with their cousin in battle?" The sons of Aqeel exclaimed.

"By God, we could never," said the sons of Muslim ibn Aqeel. "We will give our lives, our wealth, and our family for you, Uncle Husayn! We shall fight alongside you until we reach our fate with you, and may life be misery if we are to live after you!"

From amongst a group of companions that sat around a fire, Muslim ibn Awsaja stepped forward, extending his hand towards Husayn. "Shall we forsake you, O Master?" Muslim asked with a tear in his eye. "How could we stand before our Maker after leaving you? What would we say to our Lord on that day?" Some of the companions began to weep at the words of Muslim. He grasped his spear with his right hand. "Nay!" Muslim bellowed. "I shall pierce this lance of mine in the hearts of your enemies. And I shall strike them with my sword until only its hilt remains in my hands," Muslim roared as his companions readied their sharpened swords. "And if my weapons are taken from me, I shall attack them with these bare hands! I swear by God that we will not leave you until we bring you honor!" Muslim proclaimed.

"We will bring you honor!" the men cried out in unison.

Zuhayr continued the proclamation with a phrase so profound, it would echo for eternity:

"It would be my life's honor that I be killed and rise again, a thousand times over, by your side, my master, Husayn," Zuhayr said solemnly, kneeling before his Imam.

"A thousand times over." The companions pledged.

Husayn took in the scene and nodded. "Then tomorrow, my companions, we shall all be martyred together," Husayn looked on as he embraced Zuhayr and Muslim.

From amongst the family, a young warrior stepped forward. It was Qasim ibn Hasan, Husayn's nephew.

"Will you give me the honor to be amongst those martyrs, uncle?" Qasim asked eagerly.

Husayn turned around to see his young nephew. Moved by his demeanor, he asked Qasim, "And how do you see this death that you ask about dear nephew?

"To die for you is sweeter than honey to me," Qasim replied, smiling.

"May I be sacrificed for you my son," Husayn replied. "Indeed, you will be amongst the martyrs."

"Praise be to God, for giving us the honor to die alongside you," another companion supplicated.

Husayn lifted his hands to the Heavens and prayed for his men. They bowed their heads in a moment of prayer. Some smiled, some cried, and some hymned. Husayn lowered his praying hands and told his men to raise their bowing heads.

"I want you to see where you will be in Paradise, my companions," Husayn said. They lifted their heads to gaze upon a manifestation of Paradise they could have never imagined. Before them, in that starry night, they saw their stations in Heaven. "There you are," he told his men. "Each of you in your place in Paradise."

The men gazed in awe. Tears of joy ran down their cheeks. The honor and the reward were overwhelming. Tomorrow's tragedy would be their gateway to blissful salvation.

After the companions gazed upon their stations in Heaven, Husayn gave them a task. He ordered them to dig a trench around their camp and fill it with firewood.

As the men went out on their task, Husayn returned to his tent and prepared for tomorrow. A man named John accompanied Husayn to help him. He sharpened Husayn's sword and readied his armor and shield. John was the servant of Abuthar al-Ghifari, a loyal companion of Husayn's father, Ali. As John sharpened Husayn's sword, Husayn lamented time:

> *Time, shame on you my friend*
> *As the day dawns and the sun sets*
> *How many a seeker will be a corpse*
> *Time will not be satisfied with any substitute,*
>
> *But the matter will rest with the Almighty One,*
>
> *And every living creature will have to journey*
> *They will walk along my path*
> *They will sing my sorrow.*

When the trench was dug and the firewood was brought, Husayn left his tent and gathered his companions once again. "This will be our final night," Husayn said. "Prepare yourselves… These clothes you wear will be your shrouds. Tomorrow, will be our last day."

The rest of the night was spent in quiet prayer, repentance, and supplication. As Husayn continued to lament time through his couplets of poetry, his son Ali Zayn al-Abideen was in the background listening. He was heartbroken at the sight of his father. Though Paradise did await them, the tragedy was overbearing, even for the most forbearing of men.

Zaynab also heard the lamentation of Husayn, as she tended to her ill nephew, Ali. It pained her so deeply. Though she knew like everyone else of the fate they faced, it was nevertheless a piercing spear in her heart. Husayn was her everything, and tonight would be her last with him.

Zaynab rose from Ali's bedside and came closer to her brother. She sat beside him with tears in her eyes. She touched Husayn's shoulder.

"Together, we lost our mother, Fatima, as children," said Zaynab as she gazed at him. "We grew in the shadow of patience that was our father, Ali. Then he was taken from us. Yesterday, we lost our brother, Hasan. And now, you are going to join them?"

"This is my fate, dear sister," Husayn replied.

"You are the successor of those departed and the hope of the ones who remained. If you leave, I pray that I am taken with you brother."

"Dear Zaynab, you have to be the mountain of patience that you are," Husayn replied with tears in his eyes. "For the women, for the children, for them all."

Zaynab nodded silently as she wiped away her tears.

Husayn looked off and said somberly, "If a bird is freed at night, it will sleep in peace."

Before dawn, Husayn briefly rested his head and dozed off. It was only minutes that his eyes would close, but he awoke invigorated. He leaped from his cot and went outside to find his companions and brothers gathered.

"Do you know what I just dreamt?" Husayn exclaimed as he entered their circle.

"What have you seen, master?" they replied excitedly.

"I was alone. Surrounded. Not by men, but by dogs. The dogs attacked me, growling, barking, and gnawing at my flesh. One dog, a piebald sort, was especially fierce. That one would not let." The men's eyes grew wide as Husayn recounted his dream. "Then I saw my grandfather, the Prophet of God, along with my father and his companions," Husayn said. Their faces illuminated brightly. "The Prophet would come closer to me with his immaculate smile. He said to me, 'My son, you will be the Martyr of my Progeny. The one who will kill you will be a leper among this nation.'"

The men's faces turned somber at the thought. They were protective of their leader. Though he embraced his own fate, it continued to pain them.

"My grandfather continued, 'The dwellers of the heavens and the heavenly Angels give glad tidings to you. Tonight, you shall break your fast with me; thus hasten and do not delay,'" Husayn quoted the Prophet with a smile. "Truly, my end is near. It is my time to depart from this world."

CHAPTER 12

A CALL FOR PEACE

O people! Remember who I am and to which family I belong. Think to yourselves and admonish your conscience. Ask yourselves if it is right for you to kill me.

– Husayn ibn Ali

Before the battle would commence, Husayn called for his horse. One of his men hurriedly obliged and brought forth the magnificent steed. The horse had been in the family for years, ridden by his father, Ali, and was originally bought and raised by his grandfather, Muhammad. The horse's name was Dhul-Jinah – That of Wings. This horse was beloved to the family, and as the story of Karbala would unfold, it would loyally serve Husayn.

Accompanied by his loyal companion, Habib, Husayn gallantly rode Dhul-Jinah to the center of the battlefield so that all the men of Ibn Saad's camp could see him and hear him clearly. The thousands of men that stood across from him were there to kill him. Some were promised riches; others were infested with hate. They had been blinded by greed and spite. Husayn did not thirst for blood, though he ached for justice. What pained him more was the extent to which the nation of his grandfather had strayed from the path.

"O people! Listen to me and do not be hasty with me until I advise you, as that is a right of yours over me." Uninterested, the men listened to Husayn recite verses from the Holy Quran and speak of hope, salvation, and God's justice. Husayn continued, "I can see that you agreed on a matter by which you have reaped the wrath of God, causing Him to turn His face away from you, making His curse befall you, and causing Him to exile you from His mercy. The best of lords is our Lord, and the worst of servants are you! You claimed obedience to God and belief in His Messenger, Muhammad. Now you march towards his offspring and progeny, intent on killing them!"

The Prophet's grandson went on to speak of the devil's chokehold on them, how they had forgotten God, and prayed aloud against the oppressors, wishing doom upon their aspirations. Some of the men began looking at each other nervously; others stared on with indifference. The commander amongst them, Umar ibn Saad, turned towards his men angrily.

"Answer him! By God, he is just like his father! If he stands for another day, he will not stop, nor will his words come to an end!"

Shimr stepped forward from the ranks and looked right and left in disgust. He had no patience for Husayn's advice or reminders. He was amongst the anxious to receive the promise of wealth for Husayn's head.

"Husayn! What are you saying? Tell us so that we understand," Shimr bellowed into the battlefield.

Husayn's eyes fixated on Shimr. "Do not hasten against me. I have only come in response to the letters of the notables amongst you calling for me," Husayn said. "You wrote to me saying 'The traditions of our Prophet had been undone, hypocrisy has grown, and law and order has come to a halt, so come to us so that perhaps God may reform the nation through you.'" Husayn quoted the thousands of letters he had received from Iraq. Husayn stretched his arms out, gesturing to the sands of Iraq, "So I came forth and here I am." Their eyes were glued to him, and feelings of remorse began to grow in some of their hearts. But most hearts remained as they were, as stone. "But if that is not what you want, then I shall return from where I came at once."

Ibn Saad's men did not reply; the eerie silence only grew louder with the whirling winds of Karbala's desert plains. The sun's scorching rays beamed on their backs. Their armor grew heavier on their shoulders. Husayn did not accept their careless silence. So, he filled the air with the relentless weight of truth.

O people! Remember who I am and to which family I belong. Think to yourselves and admonish your conscience. Ask yourselves if it is right for you to kill me. Am I not the son of your Prophet's daughter? Am I not the son of your Prophet's cousin and vicegerent? Was my father not the first to believe in God and His Messenger who delivered to you the will of his Lord? Is Hamza, the most noble of martyrs, not my great-uncle? Is Jaafar al-Tayyar the martyr not my uncle?

Have you not heard of the words of the Messenger of God concerning me and my brother: 'These are the two masters of the youth of Paradise'? Believe what I say, as it is certainly true! I swear that I have not lied since I have known that God hates liars and punishes fabricators.

And if you deny what I say, ask the educated amongst you and they will assure you of my truthfulness. Ask Jabir ibn Abdullah al-Ansari, Abu Saeed al-Khidari, Suhail ibn Saad al-Sa'idi, Zayd ibn Arqam, and Anas ibn Malik. They will assure you that they heard these words from the Messenger of God in favor of my brother and I. Would this not give you pause and stop you from shedding my blood?

On that day, Husayn did not leave a single burden of proof unmet – even though the burden of proof to save his own life shouldn't have been his burden at all.

As the men took Husayn's words in, Shimr madly interrupted with a belligerent shout. "Soon you will enter Hellfire, Husayn!" he hollered.

Husayn calmly replied, "God is great. I recall my grandfather, the Prophet, telling me as a child: 'I saw in a vision, it was as if a dog was licking up the blood of my family.' I have no doubt that the dog is you, Shimr."

"O Husayn! You make no sense. My worship of God would be corrupt if I knew what you are saying!" Shimr yelled back at the Prophet's grandson with an unrelenting grimace.

Habib could handle these insults to his master no longer. Though Husayn did not reply to Shimr's ignorant remark, Habib slung back. "You are the Enemy of God and His Prophet! By God, I see that you worship God on seventy doubts as it is clear you do not know what he is saying! God has surely sealed your heart so that you do not understand!"

Husayn turned to the loyal Habib, still upon his horse, and asked him to remain calm. "Patience, my brother from Banu Asad. Judgment has been passed and the pen of God's decree has dried. Indeed, God will carry through His decrees." Husayn assured his companion that their hope was in God, and He was the best protector.

Husayn then looked to the Heavens and whispered, "By God, I long for my grandfather, my father, my mother, and my brother… a longing greater than that of Jacob for Joseph. Surely, I have been decreed a death that I will meet!"

Husayn turned back to the enemies before him. His whisper would elevate to a roar. His voice filled Karbala. "If you doubt what I have said, do you doubt that I am the son of the daughter of your Prophet? By God there is no son of a prophet other than me amongst you or amongst any other nation between east and west! Woe to you! Do you seek vengeance for a man I murdered? Do you seek compensation for wealth that I have damaged? Do you seek retribution for a wound I inflicted?"

He paused, waiting for a response. But the desert plains once again filled with eerie silence. He would not accept it. He came in a little closer and began pointing out the men, one by one.

"O Shabath ibn Rab'i! O Hajjar ibn Abjar! O Qays ibn al-Ash'ath! O Yazeed ibn al-Harith! Did you not all write to me asking me to come forth to save you? Did you not write to me saying, 'The fruits have ripened. The pastures have greened. The rivers have swollen. The time has come and you will find armies mustered at your command. So, come forth.'"

The men mustered some false courage and finally replied, "No we did not!"

"Dear Lord!" Husayn exclaimed. "I swear by God that you did!" Husayn's heart filled with angst, as these men lied through their teeth. These were the same men who begged him to save them from the tyranny of Yazid, and now they lingered like heartless ghosts with the devil's scent. Husayn then repeated, "If you hate me so, then let me be and I will find a place away from here to go to."

One of the men that he had just called out, Qays ibn al-Ash'ath, stepped forward, cleared his throat and muttered, "We don't understand what you're saying, Husayn!" Husayn looked on as these men continued to reaffirm their hearts of stone. Qays continued, "Will you not then come under the authority of your kin? I swear that they will only give you what you please and they will not harm you."

"The blood of Muslim ibn Aqeel was not enough, so that you have come to shed even more blood from Banu Hashim?" Husayn challenged the claim, which was, at best, naïve. Husayn pulled the reigns of his horse as it neighed. "By God, I will not pay homage in such disgrace, nor will I flee like a slave. I seek protection from my Lord, as you dare to kill me. And I beseech my Lord from the tyrant that does not believe in the Day of Judgment."

"What are you waiting for!" Umar ibn Saad called out to his soldiers. "Advance at once against Husayn; we will devour them in one meal!" Ibn Saad marched ahead of his men, placed his arrow on his bow, and released it into the skies of Karbala. He then turned to his men with a smug look. "Men, bear witness before the governor, that I was the first to launch an arrow against Husayn," Ibn Saad said.

That single arrow was followed by thousands more, as the troops launched their arrows in a single volley at Husayn and his warriors. The valiant men of Husayn's camp used their shields to protect against the pelting wave. With so many arrows on such a small band of men, however, everyone was hit. Some fell in that wave, others survived. Husayn did not want battle, but Ibn Saad's arrows initiated the inevitable.

The Devil had seized their army. He and his demons disguised themselves in the garb of men. God was merely a word uttered, and not a meaning understood. They thirsted for Husayn's blood, his companions' heads, and the devastation of his family. As the arrows rained down on them, Husayn looked at his men under his shield. They took cover and smiled at one another, as the arrows pelted their metal shields.

"Go forth, my men! Go forth to your glorious deaths, may God have mercy on you!"

The battle would begin.

CHAPTER 13

THE BATTLE BEGINS

*I am choosing between Heaven and Hell here... and I will not choose
anything over Heaven."*

– Hur ibn Yazid al-Riyahi

Umar ibn Saad's men were ready to attack. Battle formation
was set. Before the commander gave the order for the assault,
Hur rushed towards him.

"Commander, are you truly going forth with this battle?" Hur
exclaimed.

"We have no choice," Ibn Saad replied.

"What do you mean? The plan was to stop him from pro-
ceeding to Kufa, not to kill the man!"

"If it was up to me, I would do otherwise."

"It is up to you! You are the commander here!"

"I am following orders!"

"Is that so?"

"Take it up with the governor, Ibn Ziyad, or better yet, the
Caliph himself! They want Husayn dead!"

Hur nodded and returned to his tent. He paced back and forth, thoughts racing through his mind. It was a reality he did not want to face. He had a choice to make, one that could change his fate forever. Hur took his horse and began walking it away from his tent. A friend of his, Muhajir ibn Aous, watched him from nearby. He saw him leaving, visibly distraught. He did not look good.

"Hur, where are you going, friend? Taking your horse for a drink of water?" Muhajir asked. Hur turned around and looked at him blankly. He did not respond. "Hur? Are you okay?" his friend asked. Hur nodded slowly as he looked at the camp of Husayn. "Wait," Muhajir said. "Are you planning to take the charge on the camp of Husayn?" Muhajir smiled smugly.

Hur looked back at Muhajir and said, "I am deciding between Heaven and Hell, old friend."

"What do you mean?" Muhajir asked, confused.

Hur gazed at the camp of the army he came with to Karbala and exclaimed, "I will not choose anything over Heaven, I cannot."

Hur jumped on his horse and galloped towards the camp of Husayn, leaving Muhajir and the rest behind him. His thoughts continued to race, faster than his horse, faster than his heartbeat, faster.

Husayn stood outside the camp, watching, as Hur trotted towards him. Hur saw Husayn standing outside of the tents. He was larger than life. His face illuminated even in the brightest day. Husayn was nothing short of majestic. Hur jumped off his horse and kneeled before Husayn.

"Peace be upon you, Master Husayn," Hur said.

"And upon you, Hur," Husayn replied.

"I have come here to repent."

Hur began to cry. He said, "I am the cause for your pain. I am the one who stopped you and besieged your family in this unforgiving place. I am the one who brought fear into the hearts of the women and children." Husayn nodded with a smile that could not hide his pain. The man continued, "Dear Imam, by God, I am coming to repent for my sins. Is there a repentance for this lowly servant?"

Husayn touched Hur's shoulder and raised his head. "God accepts your repentance," Husayn reassured him. Hur embraced Husayn at his legs and continued to cry. He joined the ranks of Husayn's men, who welcomed him with smiles and open arms. Hur was home.

The companions readied themselves for battle. Their time had come. They each pledged to give their lives in battle before any members of Husayn's family set foot onto the battlefield. It was a matter of sacrifice and loyalty. They could not live to see a descendant of Muhammad or Ali killed before they had the opportunity to give their own lives for Husayn's cause.

In the camp of Ibn Saad, Amr ibn Al-Hajjaj was tasked to advance with his battalion of Kufans against the right flank of

Husayn's army. A force of mostly cavalry, they were hungry for blood.

"Attack them at once, Amr!" Umar commanded.

"Yessir," Amr obliged and went off with his Kufans.

Husayn's right flank was led by Habib ibn Mudhahir, the valiant companion who swore loyalty like no other. Habib saw the enemy in the distance, their horses trotting against Karbala's hot sands.

"They're coming, men," Habib told his small band of warriors who stood fearlessly, smiling in the face of death.

"Ready your spears!" Habib cried out. Gripping their spears and gritting their teeth, the men watched the cavalry get closer and closer. "Hold!" Habib shouted. The cavalry was fifty yards out. "Hold!" Habib repeated. Now twenty yards out. "Hold!" Ten yards out and the men's eyes could see the engravings on the enemies' armor.

"Spears!" Habib cried out.

Amr's battalion was within feet when Habib's men dropped to their knees and thrusted their long pikes into their ranks. The first rows were devastated by Habib's spears. Seeing the maneuver, Amr shouted from behind his men.

"Pull back! Pull back!" he repeated. Amr's cavalry pulled back on their horses, evading the pikes by a hair and retreating.

"Archers!" Habib called out to his special forces.

Habib's men dropped their spears and grabbed their bows. Within seconds, they were pelting Amr's cavalry with their arrows, killing a score of them and wounding others. As Amr's men struggled to recalibrate, he shouted at them.

"Fight these fools who have left the religion and destroyed unity!" Amr yelled.

Husayn shot back at Amr, "O Hajjaj! Do you rouse the people against us? Is it we who have deviated from the religion, while you are its guardians? When our souls leave our bodies, you will know who is truly deserving of dwelling in Hellfire."

Amr's cavalry regrouped and attacked again. The forces clashed for some time in fierce battle. Muslim ibn Awsaja was amongst the warriors leading the fight against Amr's attack. He pressed into them with a handful of comrades.

"For Husayn!" Muslim repeated as he swung his sword against his enemies.

The battle grew so fierce that a thick cloud of dust was stirred from the warriors' frenzied movements. The thick dust cloud covered the men at the heart of the fight. Though he could hear their loyal voices and valiant strikes, Husayn could no longer see them from where he stood. But then the voices were no more, and the clashing of the swords had stopped. As the dust settled, Husayn and Habib rushed towards the scene. Muslim lay on the ground, gravely wounded. He grabbed at his side and moaned in pain. Husayn and Habib kneeled to the ground beside Muslim. Husayn touched Muslim's bloodied head, as tears filled his eyes.

"May God have mercy on you, my friend," Husayn said. "'There are some among them who have fulfilled their pledge, and some of them who still wait, and they have not changed in the least,'" Husayn quoted Quran 33:23.

Habib held Muslim's hand in his own, as tears rolled down his cheeks. "Your death has taken a toll on me, brother," Habib said as he tried to hold back his tears. "But you will soon be in Paradise," Habib tried to smile.

Muslim replied faintly, smiling back, "May God give you glad tidings of all that is good."

"If I did not know that I am soon to follow you, I would have asked you to entrust me with your last will and testament," Habib said.

Muslim replied, "But I do have a will to entrust you with."

"Of course, dear friend, what is it?" Habib exclaimed.

Muslim slowly raised his hand and pointed at Husayn.

"He is my will," Muslim said as he gazed at Husayn with tears in his eyes. "Give your life for him."

"By the Lord of the Ka'ba, I will." Habib made a promise to his comrade.

Muslim's soul departed. He was gone.

Seeing another imminent attack, Husayn's companions withdrew and surrounded him and Habib as they cried over Muslim. The companions fought valiantly against Shimr and his cavalry, who attempted to devastate Husayn's left flank. Zuhayr led the left flank of warriors. They had thirty-two horsemen in their ranks. Each of his men equaled twenty of theirs. But even so, the enemy numbers were too vast.

In the attack, many of the companions fell. No matter how many enemy soldiers the brave men felled, it barely made a dent in the ranks of the thirty-thousand-man army. Yet even when only a small fraction of that was taken from Husayn's camp, it clearly showed. The companion that fell shortly after Muslim in that attack was Abdullah ibn Umayr al-Kalbi.

Abdullah was in the small town of Nukhayla, north of Kufa, when he saw people getting ready for the campaign against Husayn ibn Ali.

"Where are you heading?" Abdullah asked a young man hurrying in the street as he tried to catch up with a group ahead of them.

"I'm joining the army in its campaign," the young man responded anxiously.

"Which campaign? Against the Byzantines?" Abdullah replied.

The young man responded, "No, no. I think it's the matter of Husayn ibn Ali."

"Husayn ibn Ali?"

"Yes, he's on his way to Kufa. We are ordered to stop him. He's an enemy of the caliphate," said the young man. Abdullah thanked him and the young man went on his way.

Abdullah turned the corner and spoke to himself. "By God, I have been thorough in my fight against the polytheists," Abdullah whispered. "I hope that the reward for fighting the enemies of the Prophet's grandson is no less than what I earned against the polytheists." Abdullah rushed home to tell his wife about what was going on.

"They're going to kill Imam Husayn," he blurted as he entered their humble home.

"What?! What do you mean?" she replied startled.

"Thousands of troops are being mobilized and are already on their way to stop him before he reaches Kufa," Abdullah replied. Abdullah came in closer to his wife and placed his hands on her shoulders. "I have to get there in time to be by his side and fight for him."

She gazed at her husband with her endearing eyes and replied, "God bless you, my brave husband. You are fulfilling your destiny. I pray God guides and protects you on your journey."

"Thank you, my dear," Abdullah smiled.

"But take me with you," she said.

"Dear, we are going to battle," he exclaimed.

"And I will be by your side."

The couple set out to join the caravan of Husayn. They were welcomed with open arms. It was bittersweet. The camp of Husayn did not have much to offer them, but in reality, offered them everything. Hope. Salvation. Purpose. Light.

So, when Husayn's camp was attacked, Abdullah was eager to fight for him. Abdullah was tall, dark in complexion, and strikingly handsome. His broad shoulders and muscular arms gave him an impressive presence on the battlefield. He was not a known warrior, but nonetheless, he was ready to prove his worth and was eager to sacrifice for Husayn.

On the battlefield, Abdullah met an opponent by the name of Yasar. Abdullah cleared the path to Yasar and challenged him.

"Who are you?" Yasar asked.

Abdullah said he was the son of Umayr, a descendent of the Kalbi tribe. He recited the virtues of his forefathers and readied his sword.

"I do not know you," Yasar dismissed him. "Call Zuhayr ibn al-Qayn, Habib ibn Mudhahir, or Burayr ibn Khudayr to step forward and fight me."

"O son of evil!" Abdullah said, gritting his teeth, "Do not suppose you may pick and choose when the man before you is better than you."

Yasar charged and Abdullah charged back. Their swords clashed. Abdullah's blows were so heavy, Yasar was quickly overwhelmed. Abdullah continued to strike him until Yasar fell to the ground, wounded. In the frenzy of his strikes, Yasar's friend Salim charged at Abdullah from behind.

"The man is drawing near you Abdullah!" a comrade called out in the heat of battle.

Abdullah did not flinch. Salim swung his sword at Abdullah, but he quickly parried the blow with his shield. Abdullah then thrusted his sword into Salim's abdomen and slayed him. He killed nineteen cavalrymen and twelve infantrymen. As they watched Abdullah score a number of kills, the enemies surrounded him. Hani al-Hadrami and Bakr ibn Hai attacked him together. They overwhelmed him, severing his right arm and his left leg. They knocked him to the ground and then dragged him away from the center of battle. It was not long before they slit his throat and severed his head.

Abdullah's wife ran and watched the horrific scene from the hilltop. As they tossed his head on the sand, she ran down to pick up his limbs. She threw herself to the ground and placed her husband's severed head in her lap. She wiped away the blood from his pale eyes.

"You enjoy Paradise, my love," she cried. "I just pray that God would grant my wish to be with you."

Shimr watched her cry over her husband. He turned to his servant, Rustum. "Grant her that wish. Send her to Hell with her husband," Shimr said coldly.

Rustum grabbed a metal pole off the ground from outside one of the tents and made his way towards her. Rustum mercilessly bashed her head in with the rod and killed her instantly. On that day, Abdullah's wife was the first woman killed by Ibn Saad's men. She would not be the last.

CHAPTER 14

THE VALIANT COMPANIONS

It would be my life's honor that I be killed and rise again, a thousand times over, by your side, my master, Husayn.

– Zuhayr ibn al-Qayn

Burayr saw Abdullah felled by the enemy. He continued to fight on for him, and for all the men. Their sacrifice would not go in vain. He sang the praises of his forefathers and thrusted his spear into the enemies. They were hesitant to fight him back. Burayr was known for his valor.

"Come at me, O slayers of the believers! Come at me, O killers of the sons of the warriors of Badr! Come at me, O murderers of the family of the best of messengers!"

When Burayr heard that Husayn refused to pledge allegiance to the Caliph Yazid, he had immediately left Kufa and set out to meet Husayn at the House of God in Mecca. Burayr was a righteous man, known for his worship and for being one of the foremost reciters of the Holy Quran. 'The Master of Reciters' is what they called him in Kufa. He was a student and companion of Husayn's father, Ali, learning from him both in the mosque and on the battlefield.

On the battlefield, Yazid ibn Maaqil charged at Burayr. Burayr blocked his attack. "Burayr! How have you found what God has done to you?" Yazid asked.

Burayr replied, "God has done good by me and left you to your evil."

Yazid said, "You lie! Don't you remember when we walked together in the lands of Bani Lawthan and you said, 'Muawiya is misguided and the Imam of guidance is Ali ibn Abi Talib?'"

"Of course, and that is my view," Burayr smiled.

Yazid replied, "You and your leader were misguided then, and you are still misguided!"

Yazid charged at Burayr again. They exchanged strikes. Their swords sang clings and clangs in the chaos that ensued with the rest of the battlefield. Burayr would end Yazid's song with a monstrous strike upon his head. Burayr's sword split Yazid's helmet and reached his skull. Yazid was killed, but Burayr's sword was stuck in the man's skull. As he tried to pry it out, Burayr was tackled to the ground by Radi al-Abdi. They wrestled on the sands until Burayr bested him and sat on his chest.

Radi called out to his friends, "Help! Help! He's going to kill me!" Two of Radi's comrades turned around. One of them rushed to Radi's rescue, while the other paused.

"That is Burayr, the Master Reciter of the Mosque of Kufa!" The second gasped as his friend thrust his dagger into Burayr's back.

Burayr fell forward onto Radi. They pushed Burayr off of him. They slit his throat and killed him together. Those men listened to Burayr recite God's word weeks earlier, and now they listened to him choke on his own blood.

Hur and Zuhayr continued to fight on. They recited verses of the Quran themselves, in honor of Burayr. All the men did.

When the battle had begun, Hur turned to Husayn and said, "O son of God's Prophet, I was the first to set out against you, so give me permission to be of the first one to die for you." Hur bowed his head before Husayn and continued, "Perhaps that would grant me the honor to kiss the hand of your grandfather Muhammad on the Day of Judgment."

Husayn replied, "You are of those from whom God has accepted repentance; you have my blessing if that is what you wish."

Hur was special in that his name was so consequential. Hur was hand-in-hand with Zuhayr ibn al-Qayn as they set out into the battlefield. They recited verses of resolve to protect their master, Husayn. They sang his praises and glorified God with their voices and swords. They fought back to back, protecting each other's blind spots and coming to each other's aid whenever they found themselves in trouble. They fought fiercely, a sight for sore eyes and a team unmatched. They continued like that for over an hour.

Within the thirty-thousand-man army, the enemy did not realize right away that Hur had gone. When they could not find him, they argued amongst themselves bitterly. One of Ibn Saad's men, Yazid ibn Sufyan, was so upset by Hur's treason that he pledged to kill him.

"By God, if I had seen Hur when he left, I would have followed him with my spear and killed him myself!" Yazid said to the other men.

The men were engaged in a heated battle as Hur charged valiantly toward the enemy, reciting the verses of Antarah, the pre-Islamic Arab warrior-poet. His horse was wounded at the ear and brows, with blood flowing over its face. Al-Hossayn ibn Tameem, the police chief of the new Kufan government, watched Hur poetically slay his men one after the other. Al-Hossayn looked at Yazid ibn Sufyan and scoffed.

"This is Hur ibn Yazid who you were hoping to kill. Do you think you could take him?" he said to Yazid ibn Sufyan.

"Yes," Yazid said and went off into the battlefield.

Looking for Hur, Yazid finally spotted him.

"Hur! You traitor! Fight me!" he yelled out.

"I shall," Hur replied as he walked towards him, swinging his sword in one hand. Al-Hossayn watched the duel between Yazid and Hur with his men.

"By God, he fights as if his soul is in his own hands," Al-Hossayn said without taking his eyes off of Hur. "It won't be long before he finishes him."

"How do you know?" one of the soldiers turned to Al-Hossayn and asked.

"Because, it already happened."

Hur finished Yazid with a fatal blow. He got back on his horse and continued in the fight against the other warriors. One of the enemies shot Hur's horse in the leg, hamstringing it. The horse fell to the ground in the middle of its gallop and threw Hur off. Hur flew in the air, sword still in hand, and landed like a lion pouncing on its prey.

The lion devoured his enemies. Over forty men fell at the sword of Hur. He continued to recite and taunt the enemies with his warrior song. The more he recited, the more agitated they grew. He embarrassed them. They could take it no longer. So, dozens of them turned their attention to him and ambushed him at once. They overwhelmed the brave warrior, and he could no longer stand. He fell to the sands and called out the name of Husayn. Zuhayr and the companions rushed to him and fought off the ambush. But it was too late. Hur was taking his last breaths. Zuhayr carried him off the battlefield and back to the camp where Husayn stood at its edge, watching the battle.

"A death like the deaths of the prophets and the families of the prophets," Husayn continued to repeat. When Husayn saw Hur, as he was brought before him, he wiped the blood from his face and smiled. "You are Hur, the Free, as your mother named you. You are free in this world and the next," Husayn assured him as he gently brushed his head.

Hur smiled back with all that was left in him. Though he had been in the other camp for many days, in his last hours he lived free. And thus, he died free. Ali ibn Husayn stepped forward and eulogized Hur as Husayn and the companions cried over him.

> *Glory be to Hur, the Free amongst men*
> *He was a lion in the clashing of spears*
> *Glory be to Hur, who heard the cry of Husayn*
> *And sacrificed himself this early morn!*

The men returned to battle. The enemy would not stop for them to mourn. Their arrows continued to shower upon their ranks. More and more of the companions would fall. But there were still valiant warriors left. The battle was still young.

Wahab ibn Abdullah entered the battlefield with his new companions. Like Hur, Wahab was new to the caravan of Husayn, new to the religion altogether in fact. Wahab had been a Christian living amongst the Muslims. He always admired Husayn and his family. When he heard of Husayn's movement, he was determined to join him. His mother and wife joined him as well, the former excitedly and the latter timidly.

Before he entered the battlefield, his mother's face lit with a smile. He looked back at her to bid her farewell. She said, "Go on my son, go on! Defend the son of Lady Fatima!" Wahab's mother was an admirer of the Prophet's daughter, Fatima.

"I will, and I will not fall short!" he exclaimed.

Wahab's wife stood outside their tent, looking off in dismay.

"I am off to the battle my dear," Wahab said as he embraced his wife.

She turned to him and replied, "Do you have to go?"

"Of course I do, that is why I am here," he stated.

"But we're still newlyweds, can't we spend a little more life together? Are you going to leave me a widow at this age?"

"I am not leaving you. But what is life if we scurry away from its greatest honor and glory?"

"Is that what you're after?"

"After what?"

"Honor and glory?"

"No."

"What then?"

"I am after truth, and I couldn't find it anywhere other than in Husayn and his family."

Wahab's wife reluctantly bid him farewell and wished him God's protection. Wahab charged into the battlefield, reciting verses touting his strength and valor. He immersed himself in the heart of battle. He killed scores of men and then returned to the camp to see his mother and wife again. Breathing heavily, sweat down his brow, and with some cuts on his body, he ran to his mother and wife.

"Mother, are you pleased?" he asked, almost out of breath.

"I will not be pleased until you die in support of Husayn!" she quickly replied.

"Lord!" Wahab's wife cried out. "Wahab, please do not grieve me with your death!" She held on to his armor and cried.

Wahab's mother interjected. "Do not listen to her, my son. Go back and fight for Husayn. You will die for him and you will gain his grandfather's intercession on the Day of Judgment."

Wahab touched his wife's head, smiled at his mother, and went back into battle. He continued to fight valiantly until he was overcome by a band of soldiers. They surrounded him and overwhelmed him with their swords and spears. In the heat of battle, Wahab's right arm was severed from his body. He could no longer defend himself fully, but he continued to fight fiercely.

"I am with you, I am by your side," called out Wahab's wife from behind him, carrying a steel pole.

"Wife! What are you doing here?!"

"I am here to fight alongside you," she replied.

"You must go back, my dear," he urged.

"I will not return," she replied. "I will die alongside you."

Wahab's wife had been observing the events of this tragic day. She saw Husayn as he gazed upon the battlefield, seeing his companions fall one by one. She heard his calls for help and looked on as none came to his aid. She was heartbroken. Meanwhile, her husband was out on the battlefield, fending off Husayn's enemies. How could she not support him?

Husayn saw her in the battlefield and went down himself to return her to safety. "May God reward you well as a family," Husayn said to her. "Return to the women, may God bless you."

Wahab's wife obliged and returned to the camp. Wahab faced the dozens of soldiers that wanted his blood. He fought them with every last drop.

CHAPTER 15

THEY ATTACKED THE TENTS

They can pray under the shade of our arrows.

– Shimr

As the battle raged on, Ibn Saad saw that his forces could not flank Husayn's men, because the tents were immediately behind them. He wished to remove them all and encircle them under the open sky. Thus, he gave the order to Shimr to set the tents ablaze. Shimr led a small band of cavalry to attack Husayn's camp. They reached the outer perimeter of the camp and cut one of the tents with their swords.

"Bring the fire so that we may burn these tents to the ground!" Shimr shouted. There were women and children in that tent. Terrified, they ran out screaming. Warriors of the camp immediately responded and fought Shimr and his thugs off. It was Zuhayr with ten cavalries from the left flank.

Between the battle that ensued and Shimr's attack, Husayn yelled at Shimr. "Have you no shame, Shimr? Do you wish to burn the tent of God's Prophet?"

"Yes, I do!" Shimr replied as he swung his sword.

Zuhayr blocked his strikes and shoved him away from the tents. Husayn raised his eyes to the heavens and said, "Dear

Lord, Shimr can do nothing to stop you from burning him on the Day of Resurrection!"

Hamid ibn Muslim was amongst the men that followed Shimr to the camp of Husayn. He turned to Shimr and shouted.

"That is unbecoming of you. Do you wish to garner two traits; that you incur God's torment, and that you kill women and children? By God, surely killing the men will be enough to please the caliph."

Shimr did not know the man's name. "And who are you?" Shimr replied.

"I will not tell you who I am," Hamid responded and trotted off. He feared that if Shimr knew him, he would have him punished by the authorities.

Shabath ibn Rib'i interjected. He grabbed Shimr and pulled him back. "He is right, Shimr! I have not heard a statement nor a position worse than yours! Have you become a terrorizer of women?!"

Shimr respected Shabath, so his words sat with him. Zuhayr and his men had repelled Shimr and saved the tents from the attack. Though it was unlike him, in those moments, Shimr felt shame. He grimaced and returned to camp instead of pursuing the tents any further.

When Ibn Saad saw Shimr arrive on his horse, he asked, "You're here, yet I don't see Husayn's tent blazing."

"They repelled us," Shimr replied.

"Repelled you?!"

"Yes."

"You make sure to find another way then! Prayer is upon us, and they will want to pray. This will drag on," Ibn Saad exclaimed.

"They can pray under the shade of our arrows," Shimr said.

Back at the camp of Husayn, Abu Thumama saw that the sun was approaching its zenith. He turned to Husayn as the battle raged on. "Master Husayn, the enemy will not stop," Abu Thumama said. "And you will not be killed before I die protecting you. But I would love to meet my Lord after praying behind you one last time."

Husayn smiled. "You remembered prayer," Husayn said. He then raised his head, looking to the Heavens. "May God make you amongst the worshipers on the Day of Judgment!" Abu Thumama humbly nodded his head and placed his hand on his heart. Husayn then turned to Habib ibn Mudhahir. "Ask them to halt their advance so that we may pray. It is time."

Habib rode out with two of his men to call on the enemy for a brief ceasefire so that they may pray at camp. "Men, sheathe your swords for only a moment. The time of prayer has come. We wish to pray."

Al-Hossayn ibn Numair replied, "You want to pray? For what? God does not hear your prayers!"

"Do you suppose that God does not hear his Prophet's grandson? Do you know who you are talking about?" Habib shot back.

"Allahu Akbar! Allahu Akbar!" God is great. God is great. Abu Thumama's voice echoed in the battlefield as he recited the adhan, the call to prayer.

"Ibn Saad! Have you forgotten the teachings of Islam? Would you stop your advance so that we may pray?" Habib called out.

Ibn Saad did not reply. He looked on, ignoring the calls of Habib and dismissing the call to prayer that echoed in the desert. Al-Hossayn said, "Husayn's prayer will not be accepted!"

"I see. So, Husayn's prayer is not accepted, but the prayers of drunken bastards are?" retorted Habib.

Infuriated, al-Hossayn charged at Habib while Habib readied his sword. As al-Hossayn raised his sword, Habib struck the man's horse, launching him off its saddle and onto the ground. Al-Hossayn's face was buried in the sand. Before Habib could finish him off, al-Hossayn was rescued by his men. Habib looked at them with dismay. These men knew nothing of faith or humanity. If only the Prophet were here to see this, he thought.

Habib was no ordinary warrior. Tasked with commanding the right flank of Husayn's army, Habib was an original companion of Husayn's grandfather, Muhammad. He was about twenty-seven years old when the Prophet passed. Habib memorized the Quran and relayed narrations directly from the Prophet himself. During the reign of Ali ibn Abi Talib, Habib loyally served in the commanding ranks of his army. He was a close friend and trusted confidant.

When Husayn's cousin and ambassador, Muslim ibn Aqeel, arrived in Kufa, he leaned on Muslim ibn Awsaja and Habib.

These two companions were instrumental in gathering the thousands of people who pledged support for Husayn's movement to Iraq. Things changed, however, when Yazid placed Ubaydillah ibn Ziyad as Kufa's new governor. Ubaydillah was a despotic governor and was able to quell Muslim's movement in Kufa very quickly. People were beaten, tortured, imprisoned, and killed for any show of support to Husayn's ambassador. Along with other loyalists, Habib laid low until word came of Husayn's arrival to Iraq. Upon that news, Habib and Muslim ibn Awsaja were able to escape Kufa in secrecy to join Husayn's camp.

On the Day of Ashura, Habib was seventy-five years old. Despite his age, he killed sixty-two enemy soldiers. He recited poetry as he swung his sword and slashed his enemies left and right. He sang of the virtues of his companions and the dismal downfall of the Prophet's enemies. He swept through the battlefield like a lion. In the moments after he struck Al-Hossayn's horse, Habib was attacked by Badeel ibn Suraym. They exchanged strikes, but that was only short lived. One of Al-Hossayn's men drove his spear into Habib's abdomen, forcing him to the ground. Habib tried to get up, but Al-Hossayn was ready for his vengeance. Al-Hossayn swung his sword and struck Habib on his head, killing him. They severed his head and left his body on the sand. Husayn watched as they killed his dear friend. The scene overwhelmed him.

As he looked at the body of his companion from afar, Husayn cried, "Habib, you were a man of virtue. May God reward you for your sacrifice. God, it is in you that I place my hopes of retribution for the murder of my valiant companions."

Near Habib's lifeless body, al-Hossayn and Badeel bickered as Badeel carried Habib's severed head. "I am the one who killed the man!"

Badeel replied, "Don't claim what is not yours! By God, I killed him!"

"Listen, just give me the head for now," al-Hossayn said.

"What use do you have for it?" Badeel held back.

"I will tie it to the neck of my horse so that the people could see that I helped you in killing him," Al-Hossayn replied.

Badeel was not convinced. "No, you want the prize for yourself!"

Al-Hossayn assured him, "I promise you I will give it back. I have no need for any prize you may get from Ibn Ziyad."

Badeel gave al-Hossayn the head, which he paraded amongst his comrades during the day. He gave it back to Badeel, as promised. After the battle had ended that day, and the army had returned to Kufa, it was Badeel's turn to claim the severed head. He tied it to the neck of his horse and continued to parade it around the city. As Badeel rode his horse throughout the streets of Kufa, he noticed a young man following him.

He stopped his horse and turned around. "Why are you following me?" Badeel asked the teenager.

"Did you kill the man?" the boy replied.

"Who?" Badeel asked.

"The man whose head is tied around your horse's neck."

"Oh, yes. I did. What is it to you?"

"That is my father," the boy said somberly. His name was Qasim. "Give me his head so that I may bury it."

Badeel replied nonchalantly, "The governor does not wish it to be buried, and I wish to be given a prize for it."

"Then be sure you will have a dismal end," Qasim said and ran off into the alleyways.

Badeel turned around, shrugged and continued on his way back to the army barracks. Qasim watched him from behind the corner of a building. He continued to follow him discreetly. For hours, Qasim inched behind him until he found him alone and unguarded. As Badeel prepared to rest in his tent, Qasim jumped in and took Badeel by surprise. The teenage boy, driven by passion and love for his father, was able to beat and kill the soldier. As Badeel quietly bled out on the ground, Qasim took his father's head and embraced it.

"You honored us all, father, I hope I am honoring you." Qasim escaped the barracks and buried his father's head that night.

Back on the sands of Karbala, when Husayn saw Habib fall, he was devastated. Zuhayr was standing next to Husayn when it happened. Husayn continued to repeat, "To God we belong, and to Him we shall return." The pain of the day's tragedies was enough, but to see Husayn disheartened was unbearable to Zuhayr.

He turned to Husayn and said, "May my mother and father be sacrificed for you, O son of the Messenger of God! What is the disheartenment I see in your face? Are we not on the path of truth?"

Husayn replied, "Yes, I swear by the Lord of Creation! I know with absolute certainty that we are on the path of guidance and truth!"

Zuhayr smiled and exclaimed, "Then we will not worry, as we will soon enter Paradise and enjoy its splendors!" Husayn continued to look on to the battlefield. "My lord, grant me leave to go back into the battlefield," Zuhayr said. Husayn nodded and Zuhayr went off.

It was only moments before Zuhayr had charged into the battlefield and killed twenty enemies in battle. But he quickly returned when he noticed the men standing for prayer at the camp. He did not want to miss that final prayer.

As he returned, breathing heavily and galloping on his horse, he jumped down and bowed before Husayn. "Master, forgive me. I did not want to miss this, please lead us in this last prayer before our death."

Husayn patted Zuhayr on the shoulder, looking at him and Saeed ibn Abdullah who stood nearby. "Stand in front of me so that we can pray," Husayn said. They were to guard against the showering arrows.

Saeed gladly stood before a barrage of arrows aimed at Husayn. He would leap back and forth, intercepting the arrows with his shield, though some landed on his chest and limbs. He would continue to do so until he could no longer stand. He fell to the ground. Quietly moaning in pain, he grabbed on to the arrow that pierced his chest.

"Dear Lord, only what you wish happens," Saeed prayed. "Tell Muhammad of my support and protection of his grandson, Husayn. Please grant me his company in the Eternal Abode."

Saeed gazed at Husayn as he finished his prayers. "Have I fulfilled my duty, O son of the Messenger of God?"

"Yes, Saeed," Husayn replied as he came to hold him in his arms, "and you shall walk in front of me into Paradise." Other men rushed over to make cover for Husayn as he held his companion. The arrows continued to fall on Husayn's men.

Saeed's soul departed. Husayn held his companion, who was covered in arrows – thirteen to be exact. Arrows that were meant for Husayn, but Saeed took them – every single one.

CHAPTER 16

AFTER THE FINAL PRAYER

Let our lives be taken rather than yours! Let our blood be spilled in your honor! May our souls be sacrificed for you!

– Abu Thumama

Husayn turned to his companions who followed him in prayer. He saw the cuts and wounds they suffered, the blood that covered their bodies, and the sweat on their brows. He also saw light in their faces, each beaming with hope for salvation.

"You are my loyal companions," Husayn said to his valiant lot. He then opened his arms towards the Heavens.

And this is Paradise. Its gates are open, its rivers are flowing, its fruits are ripe, its palaces are decorated, for you. All for you. The Messenger of God, and all his martyrs await you. My father, my mother, and my brother long for you. They speak of you. They wait for you. Thus, defend your faith and protect the Prophet's family! God Almighty has tested you with us! You are in proximity to our grandfather the Prophet and you are honored by us! So, defend us, may God bless you!

The men could not help but cry. The tears they cried flowed faster than the blood they shed. "Let our lives be taken rather than yours! Let our blood be spilled in your honor! May our souls be sacrificed for you!" Abu Thumama cried out to Husayn.

"By God, no one will reach you with any harm while we are still live!" Zuhayr said as he raised his sword. "We have pledged ourselves to the sword and our bodies to the vultures. So long as we are alive, we pledge to give our every drop of blood against this wretched lot. That is our victory."

Husayn nodded and said, "Go forth my friends, honor our Prophet, and take your victory."

Abu Thumama, Zuhayr, and the companions went back into the battlefield and fought with a courage never before seen. The enemies' vast numbers did not phase them. And their own dwindling count did not dissuade them. Abu Thumama faced off with his own cousin who fought on the other side. His name was Qays. Abu Thumama did not hesitate to take him on, even with all the wounds he had endured. Qays was fierce. He wanted Abu Thumama's blood. Qays despised his cousin's loyalty to Husayn and his family. As they exchanged strikes, Qays overpowered him and thrust his spear into Abu Thumama. He killed him and did not look back.

Before Zuhayr went back into battle, he stood before Husayn for the last time. He put his hand on Husayn's shoulder and recited a verse of poetry.

Husayn, you are the guided guide
We will meet your grandfather the Prophet
And Hasan and the Chosen Ali
And the Winged Man, Jafar al-Tayyar

And the Lion of God, Hamza, the Living Martyr
You will lead us to them O guided guide

Husayn smiled and put his hands on Zuhayr's shoulders, saying, "They await you. I will see you again soon."

Zuhayr went into battle and gave his life for Husayn. With every strike, he called God's glorious name. He was eventually ambushed and killed by a lot of men. As Husayn mourned over the body of Zuhayr, a band of horsemen charged at him. Nearby stood Amr Al-Ansari. He saw the horsemen ready their bows and arrows. Amr leapt in front of Husayn to protect him from their fleeting arrows. He had lost his shield in battle but that did not deter him. He took the arrows with his chest. He protected Husayn with his own body. Taking dozens of arrows to his chest, he fell to his knees and turned to Husayn.

"Have I fulfilled my duty, O son of the Messenger?" he managed to ask as his knees sunk deeper into the sand and his blood soaked his armor.

Husayn held Amr in his arms and replied, "Yes, my friend, and you are entering Paradise before me. Give my peace and greetings to the Messenger of God and tell him that I will soon follow you."

Amr smiled and his soul departed. Amr's brother was on the other side of the battlefield. He had joined the army of Umar ibn Saad. He was one of the horsemen who launched arrows to kill Husayn. He soon realized it was his brother Amr that they had killed.

"Husayn, you liar! You deceived my brother and you killed him!"

Husayn looked up from Amr's body and replied, "I did not deceive your brother, but God guided him and left you in your misguidance."

"May God kill me if I don't kill you!" Amr's brother shouted as he charged at Husayn. Nafi' al-Jumali, a companion of Husayn, quickly intercepted Amr's brother and killed him with one strike of his sword before he could reach Husayn.

Nafi' heroically took on the rest of the enemies charging at Husayn. He reached for his bow and arrow from his back and began pelting the charging horsemen with poison-dipped arrows he had prepared for the occasion. He would not miss. Every single arrow met its target. When his arrows ran out, Nafi' drew his sword and charged at the enemy, singing:

> I am the Jumali Yemeni,
> My creed is that of Husayn and Ali
> If I am killed today, I will die happily
> This is my belief, and I will soon see
> the results of my deeds and dignity

Nafi' fought valiantly. The enemies fell by arrow and sword. But as he agitated their ranks, they only grew in number. The enemies surrounded Nafi', pelting him with their own sharp arrows. He dodged some of their strikes but could avoid them no more. The enemies' arrows showered upon Nafi' like rain from the clouds. His adversaries closed in on him and struck him with metal rods and rocks. He kept fighting until they literally broke his arms. Shimr's men threw ropes around the warrior and tied him to the back of their horses, dragging him back to their camp to torture him. Shimr presented the captured Nafi' before Umar ibn Saad. Nafi's wounds were innumerous. His body was covered in blood. He breathed heavily and looked down at the ground ahead of him.

Ibn Saad looked at Nafi' in disdain and asked, "What drove you to do this to yourself?"

Nafi' smiled and replied, "God knows what I wanted." Blood from his head flowed down his face and stained his beard.

"Do you not see what has happened to you?!" one of Shimr's men yelled at Nafi'.

"I see that I killed over a dozen of your men and wounded many others. I have no regrets. If it were not for these broken arms, you would not have captured me and I would still be fighting you."

Shimr grew impatient with Nafi' and drew his sword.

"By God, Shimr, if you were a Muslim you would have feared to meet God with our blood on your hands. But you do not. So, praise be to Him who made our deaths at the hands of the evilest of his creation."

"Enough!" Shimr shouted. He kicked Nafi' to the ground. Nafi' fell on his chest, his cheek laid on the sand. He faced the camp of Husayn.

"Peace be upon you, master Husayn," whispered Nafi' as Shimr dropped his sword on the back of his neck. Shimr killed him without a single hesitation.

Husayn watched on as his companions continued to fall. He was being torn to pieces at the sight of his men. But they did not waiver. They all fought fearlessly. Though the enemy did not hesitate to kill them, they were relentless in the defense of their master, Husayn.

John came before Husayn and offered himself as tribute. He was the servant of Abuthar al-Ghifari – the noble companion of the Holy Prophet, whom Husayn saw off before he would die in exile by Uthman's order decades earlier. Though John was an elderly man, he did not hesitate to sacrifice himself for Husayn and his family.

When John asked Husayn for permission to enter the battle-field, Husayn said, "Dear John, you followed us in hopes of good fortune. You have my permission to leave and save yourself."

John was heartbroken. He fell to his knees and wrapped his arms around Husayn's feet. He cried, "How could I leave you? Could it be that in times of fortune, I eat from your food, but in times of hardship, I desert you? Master, look at me," John said, looking up at Husayn. "I am a black man with no lineage. Breathe over me in Paradise so I smell of a heavenly fragrance, my face illuminates with light, and my lineage becomes noble. By God, I will not leave you until my blood is shed for yours."

Husayn held John's hands and raised him to his feet. "You bring us honor, John. Thank you for being our companion." Husayn smiled and embraced him. John held Husayn tight, a final embrace, before charging into the heart of battle. Husayn watched as John rode his horse towards the vicious enemies in the distance. He prayed for him to fight bravely and to honor his lineage.

John entered the battlefield like a raging bull. His youth returned to him as he rode into the heart of battle. No one could stand in his way. John swung his sword and sang the praise of Husayn. It was his life's honor to serve the family of the Prophet and their companions. He did not fall until he single-handedly killed seventy men. At first, they underestimated him. But as John so quickly killed so many of Ibn Saad's men, the enemy refocused their attention on him. As they had done with his companions, they showered John with arrows. It was the arrow that struck John in the eye that brought his demise. He was thrown off his steed and landed on his head. Enemy soldiers quickly surrounded him and thrust their swords and spears into his frail body.

"Master Husayn!" he called out faintly as the men dispersed from his body and Husayn ran to answer him. Husayn held John in his arms and prayed over his body. His soul had departed before he arrived.

"O God, illuminate his face, beautify his fragrance, and grant him an abode with Muhammad and his family in the Hereafter," Husayn supplicated with his hands raised to the Heavens. Indeed, John would be given all that he asked for. When they came to bury his body, and the bodies of the fallen warriors of Karbala days later, they found him different. His face was illuminating with light. His body emitted an aroma of musk. He smiled. He had a place with the Prophet and his family in Heaven.

As Husayn supplicated for John, Handhala ibn As'ad stood in front of him, shielding him against the attacks of the enemies. Handhala blocked the pelting of their arrows, the strikes of their swords, and the thrusts of their spears with his own body. As he fought, he cried out verses 40:30-33 from the Holy Quran:

> O my people! Indeed, I fear for you a day like the day of the heathen factions; like the case of the people of Noah, of 'Ad and Thamud, and those who came after them, and God does not desire any wrong for His servants. O my people! I fear for you a day of mutual distress calls, a day when you will turn back to flee, not having anyone to protect you from God, and whomever God leads astray has no guide.

Handhala recited the verses with his heavenly voice. But it did not deter Ibn Saad's men from pounding him with their swords. As he blocked their strikes, he continued to recite:

"O my people, do not kill Husayn and elicit the punishment of God, 'Whoever fabricates lies certainly fails'" (The Holy Quran, 20:61).

Husayn looked up at Handhala as he swung his sword and blocked the enemy arrows with his shield. "God bless you, Ibn As'ad! They answer your call by cursing you and your companions. What do you expect of them now after they have killed our brothers?"

Handhala spoke under the cover of his shield. "You only speak the truth! Then shall we not head towards our Lord and join our brothers?" Handhala replied.

Husayn said, "Go forth to what is better for you than the whole world and what is in it. Go forth to the Kingdom that will never perish."

Handhala smiled and said, "Peace be upon you and upon your family, O son of the Messenger of God. May God unite us again in Paradise." Handhala lowered his shield and ran towards the enemy.

 Husayn watched him charge at his opponents like a lion. "Amen, amen," Husayn repeated to himself as he nodded his head. Handhala fought valiantly, but was too overcome by the enemy and fell martyr. That did not stop him from smiling in the face of death. He walked into the Kingdom of Heaven.

The last companions left on the battlefield were Aabis and Shawthab. They both were known for their loyalty and love of the Prophet's family. As they fought back to back in battle, they realized their end was near.

Aabis said, "Shawthab, what would you like to do?"

Shawthab replied, "I will fight by your side, defending Husayn until my very last breath."

"I did not expect anything less from you, old friend," Aabis said with his big smile. "Let us send our farewell to Husayn, for the time has come. Every deed today counts, for it is among our last. Only judgment awaits."

Shawthab turned around and called out to Husayn, "May the peace, mercy, and blessings of God be upon you, Master Husayn. I leave you in God's care!"

Aabis followed him in a similar salutation. He said, "By God, there is no one dearer and beloved to me than you. If I were able to repel evil and death from you with anything more valuable than my life and blood, I surely would. Peace be upon you, Master Husayn. I say, before God, that I am a follower of Ali and a follower of yours."

Husayn placed his hand on his chest, accepting their salutations. Shawthab and Aabis returned to battle honored and fought valiantly. They charged at the enemy together. Shawthab fell faster than Aabis, but still fought heroically. Aabis mourned his comrade with the strikes of his sword. He roared at the enemies in his midst and charged at them without hesitation. Some of the soldiers of Ibn Saad had seen Aabis in battle before. Legend had it that Aabis was the bravest warrior Arabia had ever seen. He could not be fought, let alone defeated.

As Aabis charged at them, one of the soldiers shouted in fear, "This is the valiant lion! This is the son of Shabeeb! Do not dare fight the man alone." The soldiers retreated. Aabis chased them. They fled from him. No soldier dared to face off with him. His mere presence terrified them. The more he pursued, the faster they ran. Aabis grew impatient.

He cried out, "Are there no real men amongst you who will fight me?" Silence. The battlefield had not been quieter than in that moment.

"Cowards!" Aabis roared The soldiers continued to take steps backward.

"You wish to kill Husayn? Come fight me and claim your fame!" Aabis yelled as he rushed towards them. But now he did not carry his sword or shield. He tossed his weapons to the sand, opened his arms, and exposed his chest. "Will you fight me now? Fight me and claim your fame!" Aabis grabbed enemy soldiers with his bare hands and sent them crashing into the ground.

"Aabis! Have you gone insane?" Ibn Saad called out from behind the ranks of his men.

"Yes! The love of Husayn drove me insane!" Aabis replied as he fought Ibn Saad's men with his bare hands.

"The man has no weapons! He has no shield! Pelt him with your arrows and finish him once and for all!" Ibn Saad shouted at his soldiers. Even with that, they continued to run away from Aabis. He entered pure fear in their hearts. His passion was unmatched. He was mad for the cause of Husayn, for the memory of his grandfather, and for the honor of their faith.

Though Aabis bested over two hundred men that day, he too would fall. His might was quelled, and his blood would stain the sands of Karbala with the rest. For each companion, the reason for their fight was ultimately the same. It was, in the end, all for the love of Husayn.

CHAPTER 17

THE SONS OF ALI

*God be witness that the young man going out to them now is the closest
to your Prophet in looks and virtue. Whenever we missed the face of
Your Messenger, we gazed at Ali Al-Akbar.*

– Husayn ibn Ali

Husayn watched as every one of his men fell martyr at the
whims of demons dressed in the armor of men. When his companions were all slain, none but the men of his own family remained. His brothers and sons, his cousins and nephews – no
more than seventeen men from the Tribe of Hashim. They were
the sons of Ali ibn Abi Talib and his brothers, Jafar and Aqeel.
The cousins came together and bid each other farewell. The sons
of Ali were ready for battle.

The first of the family to enter battle was Husayn's eldest son
– Ali Al-Akbar. He was twenty-seven years old. Ali was a tall,
handsome man with striking looks. He captured the attention of
a room just by his mere presence. When he spoke, friend and foe
alike were in awe. The family agreed that none of the descendants of Muhammad resembled the Holy Prophet as much as Ali
Al-Akbar. Though he was his great grandson, and he had never
seen his great grandfather in the flesh, Al-Akbar looked like him,
walked like him, and talked like him.

Ali Al-Akbar came before his father, Husayn, and asked him for permission to enter the battlefield. The women of the camp encircled him and begged him not to leave. Their cries broke his heart.

"Have mercy on our forsakenness and do not rush to battle, for we do not have the power to overcome your loss," they said.

Ali Al-Akbar looked again toward his father and repeated, "Father please, give me leave."

"It is not easy to see you go, my son." Husayn replied.

Ali Al-Akbar said, "I must father, I can no longer look on as our men are slaughtered. These men want our blood, they will not have it so easily."

Husayn embraced his beloved son. He too knew it was time. He looked up to the Heavens from Al-Akbar's shoulder and raised his hands in supplication. As he pointed to the skies with his finger, he prayed.

> *My God, be witness, for a young man has come forward to them in this battle. No other man on the face of your Earth resembles your Messenger Muhammad in his looks, morals, and demeanor quite like him. Whenever we missed the face of Your Messenger, we gazed at Ali Al-Akbar. My Lord, deprive them of the blessings of the Earth. After You have deprived them, divide them into factions, tear them apart, make them into various sects, and do not ever let their governors be pleased with them! They invited us with the promise that they would aid us, but they have turned against us, fight us, and kill us.*

Moments later, Ali was on the battlefield. As Ali Al-Akbar rode his horse into battle, he raised his voice in verse. He wanted the whole army to hear him. He wanted them to remember who they were fighting.

I am Ali, the son of Husayn ibn Ali
We are of the Prophet, the most worthy
We will not submit to the son of an imposter
I will thrust this spear until it breaks you
The strikes of my sword will not stop
I am Ali, the son of Husayn ibn Ali

Layla came out of her tent to watch Ali ride into battle. She and her husband, Husayn, watched their son, and Husayn turned to Layla and told her to pray.

"I want you to go to your tent and pray for Ali. Ask God to bring our son back to us safely. Surely, the prayers of a mother for her son are heard and accepted."

Layla nodded her head and went back to her tent to pray. She sat in the tent alone and prayed with all her heart. She raised her hands and supplicated. "My Lord, you were the one who returned Joseph to Jacob, you brought Moses back to his mother, you protected Ismail for Hajar. I ask you by the right of Husayn and his thirst, I ask you to protect my son Ali and bring him back to me safely."

Ali fought valiantly against the enemies until the Kufans became distraught by the amount of them he had killed. Despite his thirst and the scorching heat of the sun, Ali killed 120 men. The enemies were mesmerized with his every strike and every blow, with every move and every gallop. They could not tell whether they were fighting Husayn's son or his grandfather, Muhammad. His likeness was astonishing. After killing over a hundred men, Ali rode back to his camp.

He descended from his horse to greet his father, who waited for him with open arms. "You are back, my son!" Husayn exclaimed as he hugged him. Ali was wounded but he carried himself without a display of pain. The thirst was unlike any wound, however.

> O father, forgive me, but this thirst is killing me, and the weight of my armor has exhausted me. Is there means by which I can get a sip of water to strengthen me against my enemies?

Husayn wept and said, "My son, it saddens Muhammad, Ali, and your father that you call them but they do not answer you and that you plead for their aid but they do not aid you. Surely, I hope that night does not fall before your grandfather gives you out of his overflowing cup a drink after which you will never thirst."

Ali then returned to battle. He continued to fight until he killed an even two hundred men. The soldiers grew frustrated.

One of the men turned to his comrade and said, "May I bear all the sins of the Arabs if I do not bereave his father by killing him." His name was Murra.

Murra maneuvered around Ali and struck him with a spear from the back. Ali gasped for air with the blow. The son of Husayn was then struck on the top of his head. Men continued to strike him with their swords, so he held on to the neck of the horse. The horse was disoriented with blood splattered in his eyes. The horse carried Ali straight into the enemy camp. They tore him to pieces with their swords and spears.

When his soul was about to leave his body, he called at the top of his lungs, "O father, I see my grandfather, Muhammad. I am about to drink water from his hand. He says, 'Make haste, for there is a cup waiting for you, too.'"

Husayn reached his son while he still had a breath in him. Ali Al-Akbar opened his eyes and said, "Father, I see the doors of the heavens open and the servants of Heaven are descending with cups of water, calling me to Paradise. I ask you to instruct the women not to scratch their faces in mourning me."

He then became still, and his voice became quiet.

Husayn put his son's head on his lap and wiped the blood from his mouth. He would kiss him and say, "My son, may God curse a people who would kill you. What audacity do they have against God and His Messenger!" His eyes drowned in tears as he said, "My son, you have gained comfort from the troubles and tribulations of the world, and have reached a place of ease and abundance. Your father remains, but will surely follow you soon."

Husayn took deep, heavy breaths. He cried at the top of his voice and the women began to weep. He came back to the camp, carrying his son's body.

"Carry your brother," Husayn somberly told the young men gathered in front of the camp.

After bringing back the body of the slain Ali, the sons of Muslim ibn Aqeel – Abdullah and Muhammad – charged into the battlefield. They fought valiantly until they too were slain. Upon their death, their uncles – Jafar, Abdulrahman, Abdullah Al-Akbar, Musa – all sons of Aqeel ibn Abu Talib, would rise for battle. Hasan II, the son of Hasan ibn Ali, joined the group who set out into the battlefield in a single push.

Husayn called out to them, "Be patient in the face of death, dear cousins. By God, you will never experience meekness after this day!"

Together, the group of Hashimites killed hundreds of men before they were all martyred. Hasan II was wounded, his right hand was severed, but he was not killed. He survived to tell the tale of this tragedy along with the other survivors of the massacre.

After them, Ibrahim ibn Husayn stepped forward unto the battlefield, reciting verses of poetry written in honor of his father. He charged the enemies, killing fifty cavalrymen before being killed. Then Ahmad ibn Muhammad al-Hashimi stepped forward, declaring in verse his intent to defend Imam Husayn. He charged the enemy and fought valiantly until he killed eighty cavalrymen before being killed – may God be pleased with him.

Lady Zaynab's son, Muhammad ibn Abdullah, stepped forward. He embraced his mother before entering the battlefield and made his way. He fought and killed ten enemies, but was finally attacked and killed by an enemy soldier named Amir al-Tamimi.

Watching his brother give his life in battle, Aoun stepped forward. He kissed his mother Zaynab's hand and went out. He fought valiantly. Aoun killed three cavalrymen and eighteen infantrymen. He was attacked by Abdullah ibn Qutba al-Taei, who took Aoun's life on the plains of Karbala.

Abdullah al-Akbar ibn al-Hasan, Qasim's brother, set out unto the battlefield, reciting battle verses adapted from the poetry of his grandfather, the Commander of the Faithful. He fought until he was slain. He had been recently married to his cousin Sukayna bint Husayn at the time of the Battle of Karbala.

After the martyrdom of Abdullah al-Akbar, his brother Qasim came forward. It is said that he was only a teenager, but the young man's courage was beyond his years. When Husayn saw him come forward, he embraced him and they both cried. Qasim asked his uncle for permission to enter the battlefield, but his request was denied repeatedly. The young man continued to beg his uncle for permission. He kissed his hands and feet. Finally, Husayn conceded. Qasim stepped forward unto the battlefield with tears running down his cheeks as he recited in verse:

> *If you do not know me, I am the son of Hasan,*
>
> *The grandson of the chosen Prophet*
> *And this is Husayn like a ransomed captive,*
>
> *He is surround by a wretched people*
> *May the sky never rain its mercy upon them!*

He fought valiantly until he killed thirty-five men. Qasim approached Umar ibn Saad from a distance and called out, "O' Umar, do you not fear God? Has your heart been so blinded that you do not heed God's wrath? Do you not take account of the rights of the Messenger of God?"

Umar replied, "Enough with your pride! Why do you not just obey Yazid?"

"May God not reward you for any deed! You claim Islam while the household of the Messenger of God are thirsty, and the world grows dark in their eyes!" Qasim replied.

The enemies watched him and grew in awe for the light in his face. "His face shines like the moon," Hamid ibn Muslim could not hold himself back from saying to the soldiers in his midst. He continued to stare at him in awe. Qasim realized the strap for his left sandal had been torn. He refused to walk barefoot, as doing such would be a sign of disgrace. The young man kneeled down to fix his sandal.

Amr al-Azdi turned to the awe-inspired Hamid and said with spite, "By God, I shall assault him!"

Hamid replied, "And what do you hope to achieve by this? By God, if he were to strike me, I would not extend my hand to strike him back. Leave him, for those who have gathered around him will be enough."

Amr did not care for Hamid's words. He reasserted, "By God, I will do as I said." He charged at Qasim and did not stop swinging until he was able to strike him on his head with his sword. The young man fell on his face and called out.

Uncle Husayn!

Husayn charged toward them, tearing through enemy lines like an angered lion. Husayn struck Amr ibn Saad ibn Nufayl with the sword. Amr guarded against the blow with his forearm, leaving his arm severed at the elbow. He cried so loud that the entire camp could hear him. Husayn moved back away from him while the Kufan cavalry approached, trying to save Amr. But as the cavalry charged, the horses hit him with their chests and trampled him under their feet, killing him instantly. When the dust settled, Husayn stood at Qasim's head and cried.

Away with the people who have killed you! Who is their adversary on the Day of Judgement other than your grandfather and your father? By God, it saddens your uncle that you should call him while he cannot answer you, or that he answers but cannot help you, or that he helps but cannot suffice you. By God, our voice is one opposed by many and supported by few!

Husayn carried Qasim, putting Qasim's chest to his. His feet dragged on the sand as Husayn embraced him. He carried him until he placed him with his son Ali al-Akbar and the rest of the fallen from his household. He raised his eyes to the heavens and prayed.

"My God, mark their numbers, kill them off bit by bit, do not leave any of them out of your punishment, and do not ever forgive them." Husayn then turned to family and cried out, "Be patient, my cousins! Be patient, O members of my family! By God, you will never experience meekness after this day."

Husayn's brothers then stepped forward, intent on dying in his service and protection. The first to rush into the battlefield was his brother Abdullah ibn Ali. His mother was Layla bint Masood of the Nahshal clan. He rushed into the battlefield declaring in verse his lineage and his intent to die for his brother Husayn. He continued to fight until he was killed by a man named Zajr. Husayn's brother Umar charged at Zajr and killed him with the strike of his sword. Umar's mother was known as Umm Habib. He rushed toward the enemies, swinging his sword with might and valor while taunting his enemies with prideful verses. He continued to fight until he too was killed. Their younger brother Muhammad al-Asghar set out unto the battlefield and fought until his inevitable death.

When al-Abbas saw the great number of family members who had been martyred, he turned to his full brothers – Abdullah, Jafar, and Uthman. Their mother was Fatima bint Hizam ibn Khalid al-Kilabiyya, known as Umm al-Baneen. Umm al-Baneen had raised her sons from childhood with the spirit of servitude to their older brother Husayn. Abbas looked at his younger brothers and reminded them of their duty. He made his command clear.

> O sons of my mother, step forward so that I can see you
> be faithful to God and His Messenger. You have no children that wait for your return. You have lived your
> whole lives waiting for this day. Go forth and make our
> mother proud!

The first amongst them to step forward was Abdullah al-Asghar. He was twenty-five years old. He taunted the enemy with verses in praise of his father Ali ibn Abi Talib. He fought Hani ibn Thubayt, who overpowered and slayed him. The youngest of the three, Jafar ibn Ali, went into the battlefield. He was nineteen. He too was killed by Hani, who severed his head and returned to the camp with it as a prize. Their brother Uthman, who was twenty-one years old, then stepped forward like his brothers had done before him. He recited verses of poetry in praise of his father, Ali, the Prophet, and his brother Husayn. Khawli ibn Yazid al-Asbahi shot him with an arrow to the forehead, knocking him off his horse. A man from the clan of Aban ibn Darim charged at him and killed him, returning with his head. The sons of Ali killed many from the enemies, but all eventually would fall on the sands of Karbala.

Husayn's cousins, sons, and brothers all gave their lives. Only one remained with Husayn. It was his brother, the full moon of their tribe, Abbas.

CHAPTER 18

HUSAYN'S BACK IS BROKEN

I smile in the face of death, as it reaped the souls of my brave men. I too will give my soul for Husayn, for I am Abbas and I will return the trust. I have no fear in battle, I have no pain.

– Abbas ibn Ali

Husayn and Abbas returned from the hilltop upon which they watched their sons and brothers fall. One after the other, the sons of Ali would perish. Glad tidings of Heaven, they were given; but their loss was just as painful, nonetheless. Growing tired of the painful scene, Abbas turns to his brother, Husayn.

"I grow impatient with these hypocrites," Abbas said. "I wish to seek redress against them."

"Be patient, brother," Husayn replied. "I cannot do without you. You are my flagbearer."

"Let me enter the battlefield, so that I may be your shield. Let me show them who the sons of Ali really are, I will make them scatter all near and far," Abbas exclaimed.

Husayn placed his hands on his brother's shoulders. "Please, Abbas, I need you here." He walked away. Husayn could not bear the thought of losing Abbas too.

Defeated and unsettled, Abbas returned to his tent. He paced back and forth, shaking his head, unable to sit still. Then he heard a voice, maybe two, maybe more. He walked closer to the end of his tent to hear it more clearly.

"Water, please, we're thirsty," the children cried.

Their cries pierced his heart. He sat down for a moment, as his legs gave way to their wails. Abbas placed his head in his rugged hands, praying for a way forward.

"Uncle Abbas," one of the children whispered.

Abbas raised his head to see his beautiful niece, Sukayna.

"Yes, my dear?" Abbas asked, trying to smile.

"Give me your hand," Sukayna said as she reached for the right hand of Abbas. Sukayna placed his finger on her chapped lips.

"The thirst is killing me, uncle," Sukayna said as her voice cracked. "Just a sip of water, is that too much to ask?" When the children outside heard the slightest semblance of the word 'water' coming from inside the tent, they rushed in.

"Water? Did you get us water, uncle?" one of the children asked.

"I'm so thirsty!" another child cried out.

Abbas was surrounded by his nieces and nephews begging for water. His heart shattered into a thousand pieces. Zaynab came in, following the children. She stood behind them looking at Abbas, who sat broken-hearted, unable to hush their cries. Abbas looked up at his sister, Zaynab. In their gaze, they understood one another. They did not need to speak. A thousand words were told, without a single one uttered.

Abbas and Zaynab proceeded to Husayn, who stood at the edge of their camp, staring into the battlefield. "Master Husayn," Abbas began. "I came to you again and again asking for permission to enter the battlefield."

"Abbas, I cannot lose you now—"

"You won't," Abbas replied.

"What do you mean?"

Zaynab interjected, "The children are thirsty."

"I will go to the Euphrates and fetch water for the children," Abbas said. "And I will return to the camp just the same."

Husayn turned to look at the children behind Abbas. Their eyes had sunken, their skin was pale, and their limbs were weak. They could not survive the heat any longer, none of them could.

"To the river and back?"

"Yes," Abbas assured Husayn.

"Bring the children water then," Husayn said.

Abbas was elated. He rushed to grab his sword, his flag, and most importantly, his waterskin. Abbas ascended his horse and began to make his way.

"Uncle!"

Abbas turned around. It was Sukayna trailing behind him.

"Yes, my dear?" He replied.

"Where are you going?" She asked.

Abbas got off his horse to embrace his niece. "I'm going to get you what you've been asking for, my love," Abbas replied, smiling.

"You're going to get us water?" Sukayna said, overjoyed.

Abbas nodded as he continued to smile.

"You calm the children until I come back, okay?"

Sukayna nodded excitedly.

Abbas gently brushed her head with his palm and went off. As the flagbearer of Husayn's army, and the only warrior left, Abbas continued to hold on to the flag. He strapped the water-skin across his chest and rode off with his sword in hand. Husayn watched him as he rode off into the horizon of enemy lines. There were four thousand soldiers standing guard on the shores of the Euphrates River. Their instructions were clear. Husayn's people were to remain thirsty. Man, woman, or child – it made no difference.

Abbas did not attack the men that stood before him. He spoke to them. He warned them of God's wrath. "Save your-selves," he advised. But his words fell on deaf ears.

"Umar!" Abbas roared. "Umar ibn Saad!"

Ibn Saad stepped forward to hear Abbas.

"You see Husayn," Abbas pointed back at the camp, "The grandson of God's Messenger is amongst us. You have killed his friends and his family. His children are terrified and dying of thirst. Give them some water to quench their burning hearts! He told you he did not want this battle with you. He told you again and again, 'Let me go to Rome or India and leave Hijaz and Iraq to you.' So, let the man and his family be…"

Ibn Saad did not reply to Abbas. His silence was deafening. His men, however, did reply. Some with tears and others with shrugs. The words of Abbas had indeed moved Ibn Saad's soldiers, but Shimr would make sure to dry out those droplets of empathy quickly.

Shimr called out, "O son of Ali! Know this well, that if the face of the Earth was all water and under our control, we would not give you a single drop unless you pledged allegiance to Yazid!" Shimr's men shouted in agreement.

Abbas turned his focus from Shimr and his men to the running waters of the Euphrates. If they would not give him water to deliver to the children, Abbas would be sure to take it himself. He pulled on the reins of his horse. It neighed and shifted direction. Toward the river he would ride. Toward the river his valiant steed would race. Four thousand soldiers stood guard, protecting the river from Husayn's men.

As they saw Abbas riding towards them, their archers immediately began launching their arrows. He took cover under his metal shield and dodged the hundreds of arrows that pierced through the air. Abbas was not fazed by their numbers. Instead, it invigorated him. Units from the river guard would attack Abbas by cavalry. He felled every man in those assaults. He needed not more than one swing of his mighty sword. And as he swung that sword of his, he raised the banner of God for all to see. It waved majestically over the head of Abbas. It was a sight to be seen. Mesmerized by the majesty that was Abbas, and the glory of his flag, some of the soldiers couldn't tell who was this warrior that they stood below. With every move and every gallop, Abbas resembled the brother of the Prophet – the Lion of God, his father, Ali ibn Abi Talib.

Abbas continued to pierce through the enemy lines, devastating dozens of their warriors. They knew that hundreds more could have been devastated by the hands of Abbas, but he was not there to fight them. His objective was clear. His orders were plain: to get the water for the children and return to the camp just the same.

The champion would finally make it to the shore of the river. The enemies dispersed and Abbas had a moment to breathe. He jumped off his gallant steed and kneeled down to the water. It was crystal clear and as cold as snow. Abbas dipped his hands in the river and cupped some water to drink. As he stared into the clear water in his palms, he remembered his brother, Husayn. He thought of his thirst, his pain, his tragedy. Abbas opened his palms and let the water flow back in the Euphrates. He could not drink. Instead, he spoke to himself.

> *O Self, you are nothing*
> *Without Husayn*
> *So how dare you rest and drink*
> *When he is nearing his end?*

By God, I shall remain thirsty
This is my fate, my destiny

Abbas filled the waterskin and got back on his horse. Back to Sukayna and the children, Abbas would ride, back to Husayn, his pride and joy. But the enemies awaited Abbas. He beat them to the river, but they could not let him beat them back to Husayn. As soon as his horse galloped away from the river, they attacked him from every direction. They did not stand a chance against Abbas. His single strike would fell a dozen men, as he sang his glorious song:

I smile in the face of death
As it reaped the souls of my brave men
I too will give my soul for Husayn
For I am Abbas and I will return the trust
I have no fear in battle, I have no pain

Seeing that their numbers could not deter Abbas, two of Ibn Saad's lieutenants hid behind palm trees. They waited for the right moment to attack Abbas from behind as he was preoccupied with other soldiers. The malicious lieutenants were Zayd ibn Raqqad and Hakeem ibn Tufayl.

Zayd crept up from behind his tree and took quiet steps toward Abbas as he fought off a dozen men. Abbas had descended from his horse, charging against the lot of men on foot. Zayd struck Abbas and severed his right arm. But Abbas did not stop. Losing his arm did not faze him. He took a spear in his left hand and continued to fight on.

You may take my right hand
But I will continue to fight for my faith
I fight on for the Imam of Truth
I fight on for the grandson of the Holy Prophet

Abbas felt no pain. He could not. His mind was set on getting the water to Sukayna and the children. As Abbas thrust his spear into one of the men, Hakeem attacked Abbas from the left and severed his spearing hand. Abbas stood there with no arms. As the enemies closed in on Abbas and the arrows rained down on him, Abbas had a moment to himself.

O self, do not fear this lot
Rejoice with God's grace
You are soon to be with the Prophet
And the noble and pure souls
The wretched have severed my left
O' Lord, damn them to Hell!

The enemies launched their arrows and thrust their spears. Abbas would not go down; even with severed arms he continued to fight. He lowered his shoulder and barged the soldiers on foot. While his severed hands lay on the sands, he kicked the charging men straight in their chests and sent them crashing to the ground. But their arrows would not relent, and with no arms, Abbas could not hold a shield to block them.

Abbas dodged all that he could dodge, but with hundreds of arrows falling, a few were bound to meet their target. An arrow struck Abbas in the chest. It had just missed his heart. He groaned and continued fight. His focus was clear as that Euphrates water. Return to the camp and quench the thirst of the children. Severed arms, an arrow to the chest, nothing but death would stop him from achieving that. But what if the water was no more?

Another arrow struck Abbas, but somehow it did not hit his body. That arrow pierced the waterskin he had strapped across his chest and held so close to his heart. It contained Sukayna's water, which he had fought thousands of soldiers to procure. But now Abbas looked down and watched that water flow on to the sand. There was his devastation. There was his heartbreak. There, Abbas was crushed.

Abbas's whole body froze as he watched the water pour on to the sand. The enemies watched Abbas just the same. They saw what had happened. They realized what finally broke him. And now it was time to finish him off. One of their men crept up from behind Abbas, as his heart poured on to the sand, and grabbed a metal pole. He struck Abbas on the head and Abbas would finally fall. As his chest hit the ground and his cheek touched the sand, he called out, "Husayn!"

Abbas's cry filled the battlefield. There was not a soul that did not hear him on that day. Upon hearing Abbas, Husayn charged toward the scene like a relentless lion. The lot of soldiers that encircled Abbas scattered as they saw Husayn approaching. Husayn jumped off his horse and took quiet steps toward Abbas. The dust settled. Abbas felt his steps through the vibrations of the sands. He heard his movement. His senses were heightened.

"O man that approaches me, spare me a few moments. I wish to see my brother Husayn before I die."

Husayn began to cry at the sight of his armless brother. He found him lying on his chest with arrows in his back. His eyes were covered in blood, like the rest of his body. Husayn kneeled down and held Abbas in his arms.

"Brother Abbas, it's me," Husayn said as his voice cracked.

Abbas smiled, "My dear brother Husayn, wipe away the blood from my eyes so that I can see you."

Husayn sobbed as he looked at his armless brother, wiping away the blood from his eyes. "You are the light of my eyes, Husayn," Abbas repeated.

Husayn took Abbas's head and placed it in his lap. Husayn brushed his head with his hand, trying to comfort him in his last moments.

Abbas began to weep. "How do I allow myself to be comforted by your embrace? How do I rest my head in your lap? In an hour, when you are all alone, who will lift your head from the ground and wipe the sand off your face?"

Husayn embraced Abbas again and held him tight. They cried together. Husayn tried to lift Abbas off the ground, but Abbas would not let him.

"Leave me here, brother," Abbas said.

Husayn replied, "Let me take you back to the camp, Abbas."

"I cannot go back." Abbas stated.

"Why not?" Husayn asked.

"I cannot bear the look on Zaynab's face if she were to see me like this," Abbas replied.

"What about the children, Abbas?" Husayn asked.

"Please do not take me back to the children without the water," Abbas cried. "I promised them I would bring them water. I promised Sukayna. I promised her I would get–"

"Okay, my brother, okay," Husayn calmed Abbas's cries and caressed his face.

Though they cried together, Husayn would soon be alone. Abbas would take his final breath and his soul departed. Husayn watched Abbas's soul leave his body, calling out his brother's name. *Abbas. Abbas. Abbas.*

"Now my back is broken!" Husayn cried out against the desert wind.

CHAPTER 19

FAREWELL, MY CHILD

O people, if I fight you and you fight me, what is the crime of this child that you deny him water? If you will not have mercy on me, then have mercy on this child!

– Husayn ibn Ali

Husayn watched as every one of his men fell martyr at the whim of the demons that were dressed in the armor of men. He saw his brothers, sons, and nephews fight valiantly yet ultimately slaughtered by Ibn Saad's men. Husayn ached as his loyal companions gave their lives, one after the other, in defense of him and their sacred faith. Their widows wailed and the orphans cried, echoing in Husayn's ears. He stepped out of his tent and faced the battlefield, peering upon the sands stained by his men's blood. He took a deep breath and cried out to anyone that could hear.

"Is there a defender who will defend the sanctity of the Prophet's family? Is there a believer in God who fears Him and will stand with us? Is there a supporter who will seek God by helping us? Is there an aide who will seek the rewards of God by aiding us?" Husayn called out with a voice so loud it echoed across the entirety of Karbala.

It would seem from the silence that no one would reply to Husayn's call. Husayn continued to gaze at the horizon, at the thousands of enemy soldiers that remained, and at the bodies of his fallen men. No one was left.

"Come back, my son!" Husayn heard his sister Um Kulthum call out behind him.

Husayn turned around and saw his ill son, Ali, Zayn al-Abideen ('the Best of Worshipers') had left his tent. The young Ali had fallen severely ill on the journey to Iraq, and could not stand to his feet, let alone fight in battle. But there he was, walking towards his father, supporting himself with a cane with one hand and dragging his sword in the sand with the other.

"My dear aunt, let me be," Ali said. "Leave me to fight for my father, the grandson of the Prophet."

A young man in his twenties, he saw his brothers and cousins die one after the other for his father's divine mission. He was pained by his illness not solely due to its physical agony but more so the inability to fight for this cause. That was divine will, however.

"My son, you must go back," he told Ali as tears filled his eyes.

"You are not alone, father, I am here to answer your call," the young Ali replied.

Husayn embraced him and they cried together. It would be the last embrace Zayn al-Abideen would have with his father. "Um Kulthum, take Ali back and make sure he does not leave his tent," Husayn said to his sister as he embraced his son. "This is so the earth is not deprived of Muhammad's chosen successors."

Um Kulthum put her arms around her nephew and returned him to his tent to rest. Husayn turned his face once again toward the battlefield. It was time.

Husayn cloaked himself with the Prophet's mantle above his iron armor. His legendary sword hung at his waist, his shield of steel on his back, and impeccable faith in his heart. His sisters and daughters gazed at him as he brought light to their day, like a majestic sun to its blue sky. Though his fate was soon to be death, they could not but admire how alive he made them. They lived through him and by his love. Life would never be the same after him.

"O Um Kulthum, Zaynab, Sukayna, Ruqayya, my dears… I bid you farewell, for this is our last time together. Your mourning shall begin soon after this," Husayn said to the women of the camp.

Um Kulthum ran up to him, crying out, "Brother! It is as if you have submitted to death!"

"How can one who does not have a helper, nor an aide, not submit to death?" Husayn replied solemnly.

"Then return us to the city of our grandfather!" She exclaimed.

"Dear sister, if there was any possible way for me to fulfill your wish, I surely would have." Husayn regrettably explained.

Um Kulthum lowered her head in sorrow, acknowledging the pain in his heart and the looming fate that was upon them all. Husayn placed his hands on her shoulders and smiled.

"Take care of yourself, my sister. I must go to battle," Husayn said as he wiped away her tear.

Husayn's daughter Sukayna began to wail and cry. He walked up to his beloved girl. He hugged her so tight, kissed her on her forehead, and wiped away her tears. He proceeded to lament his calamity in verse.

> *Know that your tears will flow*
> *When death takes my soul*
> *But so long as I breathe, do not sigh*
> *Do not burn my heart, with your cries*
> *When I am slain, that is the time*
> *For no one is better, than a daughter of mine*

Zaynab could not control her tears. She could not bear the sight of her brother leaving. She had just lost Abbas, and all the sons of Hashim. Will she now lose Husayn?

"O solitude! O lack of support! O dreadful end! O cursed morn!" Zaynab cried out.

Zaynab was visibly distraught. As she spoke, she pulled at her gown, tearing it. As she cried and wailed, her hair had become disheveled. The agony in her heart was unbearable. It was as if her heart was going to explode in her chest.

Husayn grabbed his sister Zaynab and embraced her. Holding her close to his heart, he whispered, "Have patience, my dear sister. There is much time for weeping." She wiped away her tears as Husayn released his embrace and began walking away from the tent.

"Wait, brother!" Zaynab called after him. Husayn turned around and gazed at his sister and the rest of the women with a broken smile.

"Stay here for a bit more, brother Husayn, so my sight can take its fill of you and so I can bid you the proper farewell after which we will never meet again in this world," Zaynab said. His daughters Sukayna and Ruqayya came in closer and held on to his arms.

"Wait here, brother, before rushing to death so that I can cool my anguish and thirst," Zaynab cried. She kneeled before him and kissed his hands and feet. The rest of the women followed suit, trying to soak up the last moments with their father, their brother, their uncle, their patriarch.

He embraced them all and continued to say his farewell. He bid them with patience and emphasized that they take care of each other. God would protect them, he said. God saw them, and He would never leave them alone. Husayn held Zaynab's face, soaked in tears, with his two palms and embraced her again.

"Hand me my baby boy so that I can bid him farewell," Husayn said to her with his broken smile. Zaynab obliged and brought him his son, Abdullah. He looked even frailer than he had earlier that day. The boy's eyes were sinking in their sockets. His limbs moved slowly, tired. His lips were dried and cracked.

As Husayn took Abdullah from Zaynab, Husayn looked up at her with concern.

"His mother, Rabab, tries to nurse him, but she is without milk. The dehydration has left her dry, it's killing her that she cannot feed him," Zaynab complained. Rabab was away in her tent crying, trying whatever she could to feed her son, but to no avail.

Husayn resolved to try and get some water for the infant. As he took Abdullah in his arms and kissed him, he said, "May God remove His mercy from these people, as their adversary on the Day of Judgment will be your great-grandfather, Muhammad."

Husayn wrapped his son around his chest and climbed onto his horse. He took to the battlefield and stopped at its center. Unwrapping his son and raising him on a hand for the enemies to see clearly what he came with, he filled the land with his voice.

"This is my son, Abdullah," Husayn called out to Ibn Saad's men. "His mother's milk has dried up, as the women have not had water in days. My son is hungry and thirsty. Is there a way for him to have a sip of water?" Husayn paused for a moment as the men began to murmur amongst themselves. "O people, if I fight you and you fight me, what is the crime of this child that you deny him water? If you will not have mercy on me, then have mercy on this child!" Husayn asserted as he lifted his son even higher for them all to see. Abdullah's cries grew louder as the men deliberated amongst themselves.

"Give the boy some water!" some said sympathetically.

"Don't you dare give water to Husayn or his sons!" others replied in spite.

For minutes, the men bickered back and forth, torn by this baby's cries that echoed in the battlefield. The men had never seen anything like this. Why would we starve a baby? What use would that do? They argued. Umar ibn Saad saw the rift this created in his army. He would not have it. Umar turned to his best archer, Harmala.

"Harmala, end the dispute at once!"

Harmala knew what to do. He grabbed a three-pronged arrow and placed it on his bow. He closed one eye, cocked back, seemingly aiming it at the valiant Husayn. He released his arrow and it went flying into the dry desert sky. But the arrow did not land on the body of Husayn. It didn't touch him, yet it hurt him more than any arrow ever would. Harmala's arrow struck baby Abdullah as he was in his father's arms. The boy fluttered like a wounded bird. Husayn's eyes grew wide as his infant's blood flowed onto his hands. They did the unthinkable. They slaughtered a baby.

Husayn held the pool of blood in his hands and raised it to the heavens. Not a single drop of that blood fell to the sand. It is said that had that blood fallen to the sand, God's wrath would have swallowed Ibn Saad and his men. But Husayn's sacrifice was far greater and his compassion ever-encompassing, that it even encompassed those who killed him. Abdullah's fluttering stopped. Husayn held his boy even closer. Just as he could not control the blood flowing out of Abdullah's veins, Husayn could not stop his tears from falling. He cried out to the heavens.

"What has befallen me is only eased because it is all in your eyes… O God, if you have kept victory away from us, then let it be for something greater. Exact our vengeance from the oppressors. Let what has befallen us in the present be our provision for the Hereafter. O God, be witness to a people who have killed the one most similar to your Messenger, Muhammad."

Husayn heard a reply from Heaven. "Worry not, O Husayn, we will provide for your boy… we are waiting for him," the angelic voice said.

Husayn came down from his horse, holding Abdullah, who had been drenched in his own blood. Husayn removed the sheath of his sword and dug a small grave. He buried his son at this scene. Fate had it that he too would have a grave in Karbala with the fallen warriors of Husayn.

On this day, men and children were killed alike. On this day, no mercy was felt, nor clemency offered. A sip of water was denied to the most innocent of God's creatures.

Husayn would turn back to the army of Ibn Saad and call out, "Woe to you! Why do you fight me? Is it for a truth that I have abandoned or for a tradition that I have replaced? Or for a divine ruling that I have changed? Why?"

After a moment of silence, one of the men gathered the courage to answer the mourning Husayn. "We fight you because we hate you. We hate you and your father for what he did to our elders in the days of Badr and Hunayn."

It was then that Husayn felt a loneliness like no other. Their spite for his father brought tears to his eyes. How could any man hate Ali, the bearer of truth? But of course, he was reminded of the Prophet's words to his father.

O Ali, only a believer could love you and only a hypocrite could hate you.

Husayn looked for the lovers of Ali, but they all had perished. His companions and the companions of his father had embraced the dust with their honorable deaths. Husayn stood alone, crying out for his fallen comrades.

O Muslim ibn Aqeel! O Hani ibn Urwa! O Habib ibn Mudhahir! O Zuhayr ibn al-Qayn! O heroes in times of peace! O knights in times of war! Why is it that I call you and you do not answer? Why do I cry out to you and you do not listen? If you are asleep, please awaken! Has your love for your Imam been shaken so that you are not aiding him? These are the women of the Prophet's family, devastated by your absence. Wake up from your slumber, O most honorable of men! Repel these evil tyrants away from the Prophet's family!

Husayn paused, as if awaiting a reply from his fallen warriors. But their bloodied bodies had already spoken a thousand words.

"Alas! By God, the calamities of the time have trampled you. This treacherous age has betrayed you. Otherwise, you would not fall short in aiding me. You would not ignore my calls! We are bereaved at your loss and will soon follow you. Indeed, we are of God and to Him we shall return…"

CHAPTER 20

HUSAYN IN THE BATTLEFIELD

I am warning you, O followers of Abu Sufyan! If you have no religion and you do not fear God, then at least be free in this world! Return to your roots if you are Arabs as you claim!

– Husayn ibn Ali

The hour of Husayn had come. The hyenas had howled outside of the lion's den long enough. The brave knight came out to defend the kingdom of God. Little did they know that Husayn had no interest in rule or power, even when he told this over and over again. He wanted only to defend the faith and ensure that truth would forever echo in the world his grandfather left behind. Husayn ascended his noble steed and charged at the enemy's right flank at full speed. His advance was as poetic as it was deadly. The soldiers braced themselves for the impact of Husayn's sword and spear. Charging at them, he roared in verse:

Death is better than life in disgrace
And disgrace is better than damnation in Hell
But God is my sanctuary from either fate

The enemy dispersed at the first sight of Husayn's charge. Fear overcame them. Anyone who continued to stand there was toying with death. And those men were not there to die. They longed for a prize from the caliphate, and death was not such an award. On that day, Husayn and his valiant men saw glory in their own deaths. To die was victory on that day. Their death would bring life to the faith and hope to the nation of Muhammad.

After felling a score of soldiers, Husayn would ride towards the left flank of the enemy's army. The knight upon his steed rode gallantly like the cool wind. As he came closer to the enemy, however, the cool wind whirled and spun. A storm was coming.

> *I am Husayn ibn Ali*
> *I will not bend to my enemy*
> *I will protect my father's family*
> *On the Prophet's path faithfully*

Scores more would fall at the sword of Husayn. The rest would retreat and scatter. Pausing for a moment after slaying his enemy, Husayn looked towards the Euphrates. Ibn Saad's army guarded that river like it was gold. Four thousand troops, between cavalry and infantry, patrolled the river. Husayn was not to drink even a sip of water – those were strict orders.

Husayn approached as thirst continued to weaken him. He called out to the men, "By the right of my grandfather, the Prophet, give me just a sip to cool my body." He knew they would have no compassion. But yet again, he provided them an opportunity to turn to God.

The soldiers laughed at Husayn, mocking him with cries of thirst. They taunted him as they raised cups filled with cold water. They drank and cheered as Husayn's body ached of thirst. His lips cracked and bled. He tried to wet them with his tongue, but to no avail. His tongue was dry like the sand, gashed, and torn. Husayn's eyes began to betray him, as dehydration was the most formidable opponent on that battlefield.

Fixed on finding a way to the water, Husayn was shot with an arrow, which struck his jaw. Amid the agonizing pain, he pulled the arrow out and blood gushed out. As he had done before, he cusped the blood with his palms and raised his hands to the heavens.

"O God, I complain to you alone as you see what is being done to your beloved's grandson," Husayn prayed.

He then turned back to the damned group of soldiers and challenged them to duel. One by one, they would try to claim their fame. But they stood no chance against the valiant Husayn. He cut them down like grass. There was no match for him. Unable to move him, a band of soldiers made a maneuver behind him circulating the camp of women and cutting him off from a path of return. Husayn saw the move and roared.

"I am warning you, O followers of Abu Sufyan! If you have no religion and you do not fear God, then at least be free in this world! Return to your roots if you are Arabs as you claim!"

"What are you saying, Husayn?" Shimr questioned.

"I say that I am the one fighting you and you are fighting me," Husayn asserted. "The women have committed no crime. Forbid your defiant, savage, and ignorant soldiers from attacking my family so long as I live!"

Shimr paused and nodded. "You shall have that, O son of Fatima," he said. The general then turned back to his men and commanded, "Leave the man's family and attack him!"

The men moved away from the camp and instead charged at Husayn while he continued to seek a drink of water.

"By my life, he is a noble opponent," Shimr muttered as he watched his men attack Husayn and fail.

Whenever Husayn approached the Euphrates on his horse, the enemy would charge at him and repel him from the river. Husayn then charged at the river battalion's leaders, Awar al-Salami and Amr ibn al-Hajjaj. He scrambled their troops and created a clear path to ride his horse into the Euphrates. At its shores, Husayn jumped off his horse and kneeled down to the flowing water.

When the horse lowered its head to drink, Husayn looked at it and smiled. "You are thirsty, and I am thirsty. I will not drink until you do," Husayn said to his noble steed.

The horse raised its head as if it had understood his words and looked back at his knight. Husayn repeated his words.

"Drink," he said as he patted its head.

The horse drank and Husayn was relieved. He dipped his two hands in the cool clear water and raised it to his mouth to drink. Before the water touched his lips, one of the soldiers behind him yelled out.

"O' Husayn! Do you savor a drink of water while your family is being attacked?"

Husayn threw the water in his hands and leaped onto his horse in a flurry. The knight and his steed charged through the enemies, striking away at the soldiers below them, clearing the path towards the camp. On his mind were his women and children. The thought of harm coming to them could kill him faster than his thirst. Faster than lightning, he rode back to the tents.

He jumped off his horse and ran towards his sisters and daughters who came outside at the sound of his neighing horse. They were elated to see their knight.

"Baba! You're back!" Sakayna called out as she ran up to hug him.

"Are you okay?" Husayn said as he held her face with his hands.

The women came in closer and he welcomed the embrace, relieved that the attack was a farce. Ibn Saad's men had not attacked the tents yet; they just wanted Husayn to stay thirsty. Husayn held his daughters tight and reminded them of their destiny.

"Be ready for tribulation," Husayn said somberly. "Know that God Almighty will guard and protect you, saving you from the evils of the enemy. He will deliver you to a great end. He will chastise our enemy with all kinds of punishments. And He will reward you for this trial with all kinds of blessings and honors. So do not grumble and do not say with your tongues anything unbecoming of you."

As Husayn consoled his family with the protection of God, Shimr saw an opportunity. Shimr approached Umar ibn Saad and said, "Commander, this man will kill us all if we continue to duel him one by one."

Ibn Saad asked, "So what should we do?"

"We should divide our troops in three; one to pelt him with arrows and projectiles, one to strike him with swords and spears, and another to attack him with fire and stones. If we do that, we will defeat him," Shimr replied. Ibn Saad liked the adjustment. So, he made the changes with his generals and gave the order.

"Men! Charge at Husayn while he is busy with his family! If you wait for him to attack, he will have you running into each other."

Husayn was getting ready to leave the camp again to the battlefield, when he saw the wave of arrows block out the sun. He rushed back to the women and shielded them with his body. As the arrows pierced through the tents and the women's veils, Husayn's daughters screamed in terror. For a moment, the arrows stopped, and Husayn checked his daughters to make sure they were not hurt.

Husayn embraced them and repeated, "God will protect you, remember what I said."

Husayn mounted his horse and took to the battlefield, away from the tents. But the farther he rode away from the camp, the more he looked back. His daughters and sisters on his mind, Husayn charged at the enemy like the lion he was. But what a gallant lion he was. He prayed to his Lord, in every strike and with every gallop.

"Lord, protect my family and save them from this wretched lot."

The enemies attacked Husayn from every direction. He charged at them as they charged at him. And in the heat of battle, one of Ibn Saad's archers scored a prize. He struck Husayn's forehead with an arrow. As Husayn's tracks slowed from the strike, the men cheered. Husayn quickly pulled the arrow out and threw it to the sand. As the blood flowed down his cheeks and through his beard, Husayn looked up to the heavens. He whispered a prayer.

"God, you see what I suffer at the hands of your disobedient and defiant servants! O God, tally their number, kill them in small groups, do not leave a single one of them on this Earth, and do not ever forgive their misdeeds!"

He wiped away the blood from his eyes with his hands and charged at the lot of men. The knight and his stallion raged at the enemy with a fury unseen. Husayn needed but one strike to kill a man on that battlefield. In those moments, he was an army all on his own. His left arm holding his shield was his left flank, and his right hand holding his sword was his right flank. His noble steed, Dhul-Jinah, was his flagbearer. Husayn was an army of one – one that thousands of soldiers would perish under. Still, the arrows and spears would rain upon this army of one.

History had not seen a man so outnumbered have stronger resolve nor a firmer heart. His sons, brothers, and companions were all killed, and still his bravery was unmatched. Men scattered before him like sheep as he charged at them so that no man stood before the lion alone. Thirty thousand men stood against one. As the day continued, Husayn killed nearly two thousand men single-handedly. The devastation was intolerable by the commander Ibn Saad.

"Do you know who you are fighting?" Ibn Saad shouted at his ranks. "This is the son of Ali ibn Abi Talib! His father is the killer of warriors and knights! Attack him with everything you have at once!"

In that moment, the archers of Ibn Saad cocked back their strings and launched four thousand arrows at Husayn. For what would seem like an hour, Husayn would cover himself with his shield, relentless in his fight. But there was only so much one man could fend off. The thousands of arrows continued to rain upon Husayn. Wounded, Husayn retreated to take a moment of rest and gather himself to attack again. They would not relent. They followed him with their spears and arrows.

Some of the men pelted him with stones, gashing Husayn's face. As blood poured from the wound, Husayn ripped a piece of cloth from his shirt to quickly dress it and stop the bleeding. Tending to himself, Husayn was struck with a three-prong arrow, like the one that killed his baby boy, dipped in poison.

As the poison entered Husayn's body, he whispered in pain, "In the name of God, I rely on God and follow the religion of the Messenger of God!" He then looked to the heavens and cried out, "O God, they are killing me knowing who I am... As I am the only grandson of a prophet left on this Earth!"

Shimr then called, "What are you waiting for? He's been overcome by the arrows!" The swords and spears of the enemy surrounded him. The men rallied around Shimr's war cry.

"Shower him with arrows!" they called out.

Enraged by their audacity, Husayn replied with strikes of his own. "You encourage each other to kill me? By God, you will never kill another of God's servants for which His anger will be greater than for your killing me! By God, I hope that He will honor me by your demise and then take retribution for my murder... Indeed, by God, if you kill me, God will turn your enmity toward one another, and you will shed each other's blood!"

The enemies increased and Husayn continued to fight back. But their numbers only closed in further and further. Zaraa ibn Shurayk struck him a deadly blow to his head. Sinan ibn Anas shot him with an arrow, striking his neck. Salih ibn Wahab al-Murri gave him a fatal stab in his waist. Husayn fell off his horse to the sands of Karbala. He fell on his right cheek. He sat up and drew the arrow out of his neck. The enemies watched as Husayn pulled another arrow that had pierced through his back. He took his blood from that wound with his right hand and wiped it on his head and beard.

"By God, this is how I will meet my grandfather Muhammad, stained in my own blood!" Husayn said. "I will say to him, 'O Prophet, I was killed by this lot of men,'" he continued.

The Prophet's grandson then collapsed, falling unconscious. He tried to stand after he awoke moments later, but his body gave out. He cried. He cried so that the heavens and earth could hear him.

> O grandfather, Muhammad! O father, Ali! O' brother
> Hasan! O Jafar, Hamza, and Aqeel! Uncles of Banu
> Hashim! O brother Abbas! How severe is my thirst and
> how few are my supporters!" Husayn cried. Will anyone
> come to my aid? Will I be oppressed and killed while my
> grandfather is Muhammad al-Mustafa? Will I be
> slaughtered thirsty while my father is Ali al-Murtada?
> Will I be left massacred while my mother is Fatima al-
> Zahraa?

No man came to the aid of Husayn, no matter how many times he cried. No matter how thirsty he was, and no matter how many arrows had struck his blessed body, no man came to his aid. But there were two boys on that day who had a resolve greater than any man in Ibn Saad's ranks. The first was Muhammad, the nephew of Muslim ibn Aqeel. He had snuck away from the women of the camp, holding one of the metal rods that held up a tent. He ran into the battlefield, trying to find his Husayn, but could not see him. Husayn had fallen from his horse and the desert dust had blurred the boy's vision.

Horsemen surrounded the boy and he suddenly found himself encircled by treacherous men. Looking to the left and to the right, Muhammad was overwhelmed and terrified. He had nowhere to go and Husayn was nowhere in sight. One of the horsemen rushed towards the boy. The evil rider leaned off of his horse, swung his sword and struck the boy down to the ground. The young Muhammad died instantly from that fatal blow.

Muhammad's eyes did not rest upon his uncle Husayn, who he wished to protect, but rather upon the sword of a treacherous man. He wasn't the only one to see the swinging of that horseman's sword. As Muhammad's mother looked for his whereabouts, her eyes spotted the movement on the battlefield. She quickly saw that the commotion surrounded her son. Unable to come to his aid, she watched her son be slaughtered by men, or rather demons.

Husayn would rise and fall time and time again, not giving in to the vastness of his enemy, the depth of his wounds, or the severity of his thirst. Every time he fell, the enemy saw another opportunity to close in on him. But he would continue to fight. He would not stop.

Zaynab, the women, and the children watched the battle from the hilltop of the camp. When Husayn was knocked down again to the ground, the women gasped and called out.

"O Husayn!"

Visibly wounded and unable to rise again, Husayn sat on the ground, trying to catch his breath. His nephew, the eleven-year-old Abdullah ibn Hasan, watched as his uncle Husayn fell. Abdullah was agonized by the sight. They told him he could not fight, because he was still a boy. He watched his brother, Qasim, who was a few years older than him, go to battle and defend their uncle's honor.

He would fall to the swords of the enemy and say, "To die with you, Uncle Husayn, is sweeter than honey to me."

Abdullah just wanted to protect his uncle Husayn, one he knew like a father his whole life. Abdullah's father, Imam Hasan, died when Abdullah was just a baby. His uncle Husayn raised him, cared for him, loved him. He could not hold himself back anymore. He had to defend his uncle, his family, his everything.

Seeing his uncle Husayn on the ground surrounded by soldiers, Abdullah ran out from amongst the women towards the battlefield. Zaynab ran after him.

"Uncle Husayn!" he called out as he ran.

"Abdullah! Come back!" Zaynab yelled.

Husayn turned to see the young Abdullah running towards him. "Zaynab, take him back!" Husayn called out, fearing for the boy's life. But the boy was too quick. He arrived at the place where his uncle sat on the ground, in a pool of his own blood.

Abdullah embraced his uncle and said, "I will never leave you uncle."

One of the soldiers came closer to them, sword in hand, approaching Husayn. Abdullah stood up to the man and reprimanded him. He stood as a young David to his Goliath.

"Woe to you! Vile man! How dare you kill my uncle?" Abdullah yelled. The vile soldier swung his sword. Abdullah blocked the strike, but he had no shield. The boy's arm was severed by the blow.

"Uncle!" he cried out.

Husayn leaped forward with all the strength he had and grabbed Abdullah in his arms. He tried whatever he could to soothe the boy with his embrace. Abdullah was in shock, as his limb was severed, bleeding out a pool of blood on its own.

As Husayn held him tight and shushed his cries, he said, "Be patient with this pain, my dear nephew, and wait for your reward with God. He will soon join you with your honorable forefathers."

Shaking and losing color in his face, Abdullah managed to smile at his uncle as he consoled him. The infamous archer, Harmala, would kill that smile. He launched an arrow at the young Abdullah as he lay in the arms of his uncle. Abdullah's breathing stopped and his soul left his body.

Husayn turned to the heavens as he had done so many times before and prayed again.

"O God, if you will provide for them for a while, then separate them into factions, make them into various sects, and do not let the governors be pleased with them. Surely, they called us to support us, but they turned against us and fought us!" Husayn lamented the tragedy his family suffered.

Zaynab could not save Abdullah. She saw him die, as she saw his brothers and cousins die. She called out across the battlefield to the commander of the army.

"Woe to you, Umar! Will Husayn be killed while you look on?"

Umar ibn Saad looked away in shame. He could not answer. He knew, more than anyone else, the crime he was committing. In the weeks prior to the campaign to Karbala, Ibn Saad spent many sleepless nights contemplating whether to take the offer of commanding the troops that would quell Husayn's movement. The task would require killing him if needed. He was no stranger to the Prophet's household. He knew the weight of the sin. Yet, he was promised dominion and rulership over the lands of Ray, a province in Iran. He had paced back and forth in his chambers, weighing his ultimate options.

"I know this decision is one between Heaven and Hell," he spoke to himself. "But I cannot let go of my life's dream to rule over Ray, I cannot!" Ibn Saad made his choice then and he reaffirmed it now. He shrugged off Zaynab's cries and the sight of Husayn holding his dead nephew in his arms. He was not backing away from his pursuit now. He was so close to finishing this.

Zaynab then called out to the rest of the soldiers, beseeching their honor as men, as Muslims. "Woe to you all! Is there no Muslim amongst you?!" They too had made up their minds. They chose their path. They were promised riches of their own. They did not respond to the Prophet's granddaughter. They paid her no regard.

Husayn lowered his head for a few moments, fatigued and dehydrated. He closed his eyes. Moments later, he saw his grandfather, Muhammad.

"Grandfather," Husayn uttered.

The Prophet smiled and extended his hand towards Husayn. "My son, have patience. Soon, you will be with us."

Husayn opened his eyes and smiled. He knew it was time.

CHAPTER 21

THEY KILLED HIM

Before you kill me, lift your mask so that I can see the face of my killer.

– Husayn ibn Ali

The valiant Husayn would finally fall. His limbs gave out, bleeding from over a hundred wounds, and suffering from severe thirst. But he would not die so simply. He lived. For three hours Husayn whispered prayers, as he lied on the sands of Karbala. He went in and out of unconsciousness as he waited for the audacious enemy that happily accompanied the Angel of Death. But for three long hours, no one dared to step forward and assume that executioner role. Each would look on to the man next to him, waiting to see who was the viler and more audacious.

In those moments, Husayn tried to appeal to their humanity once again. He asked for water. Just a sip. He had been without it for three days. His body could handle the thirst no more. Just a sip, he asked.

"You will not taste water until you reach the scorching fires of Hell!" One of the men called out. "There you can drink from its hellish boiling waters!"

"You think that it will be me who reaches the scorching fire of Hell and drinks its boiling waters?" Husayn replied in pain.

"Rather, I will reach my grandfather the Messenger of God and live with him in his home in Paradise, in the abode of truthfulness with an omnipotent King, and drink from the pristine water of Heaven."

The men looked at each other, as if contemplating giving Husayn a sip of water. He poses a threat no more. What will a sip harm us in his last moments? Some thought. But they did not speak, and the refusal remained. It was a destiny that their free will carved and sealed. Husayn would die thirsty, but he would not die of thirst.

"And rest assured that I will complain to my grandfather for what you have done to me," Husayn said as his head rested on the sand and his eyes gazed towards the heavens. Shimr walked through the men's ranks. Disgusted by their hesitation in finishing off Husayn, he grabbed and shoved any that came in his sight.

"Why are you just standing there?!" Shimr shouted. "What are you waiting for? Kill the man and finish him once and for all!"

Four men obliged. Zaraa ibn Shurayk, Al-Hossayn, Sinan ibn Anas, and Salih ibn Wahab walked slowly towards the fallen Imam. Swords and spears in hand, they contemplated how to kill him. None of them spoke. As awful as their crime had already been, they could not fathom the weight of beheading the Prophet's grandson. But they continued to walk towards the greatest sin. The gang encircled him and came in closer.

They heard him praying, repeating these words, "O God, grant us patience with your judgment. There is no God but you, O aide of whoever asks you for help." Even with all the blood and wounds, Husayn's face beamed with heavenly light. They could not look him in the eyes; they stayed clear of it. But they had to show they could carry out the task of hurting the opponent they had overcome. They gathered the courage, or rather the audacity, and closed in on the fallen Husayn.

Sinan came to his right and stabbed Husayn once in the shoulder and then again in his ribs. Zaraa moved to his left and stabbed Husayn in his other shoulder, while Salih joined the two and stabbed Husayn in his side, Al-Hossayn stayed a few feet behind them and struck Husayn's body with an arrow.

As he received these strikes, Husayn did not moan or groan. It was as if those last wounds were not felt. In the end, Husayn had been struck by dozens of swords and spears, and hundreds of arrows. And still, no one dared to come forward to actually finish him. The four men took steps back as they saw Husayn's lips moving. Was his Lord's damnation about to fall upon them? What was he saying to God now? What secrets did he whisper to the heavens? Husayn's eyes fixed on the skies as he prayed to his Lord a final prayer.

> O God, you are the Most High, you have the Greatest Power, and Most Terrible Punishment. You are independent of all creation, sublime in your glory, able to act as you wish, close in your mercy, truthful in your promise, bounteous in your blessings, and generous in your goodness. You are close if you are called upon and will

*accept the repentance of whoever repents to you. You
are able in what You will and will have what you demand. You are appreciative of those who thank you and
will remember those who remember you. I call on you
while I'm in need, long for you in my dependence on
you, seek refuge in you from my fears, cry to You in my
distress, rely on you in my weakness, and trust in You
to suffice me... O God, judge between us and our people,
for they have deceived, deserted, betrayed, and murdered us. We are the progeny of your Prophet and the
children of your Beloved Muhammad, whom you had
chosen for the message and trusted with revelation. So,
grant us in our matter relief and rescue, O Most Merciful One. Grant us patience with your judgment. There
is no God but you, O aide of those who call upon you for
help. I have no Lord but you, and I do not worship anyone beside You... so, grant me patience with Your
judgment. O aide of whomever has no aid but You! O
Everlasting who will never perish! O reviver of the dead!
O judge of every soul and what it has done! Judge between me and them, for you are the best of the judges.*

Husayn then fell unconscious. More soldiers came forward,
surrounding him, each with the damning inclination to take
part, combined with a relenting hesitation to be the only one.
About forty men surrounded Husayn as he lay unconscious.
Umar ibn Saad peered over from behind the men, seeing their
hesitation.

"Men! Finish him off quickly!" He commanded.

It was easy to say that from where he stood, some men thought. Heeding to the commander's call, Shabath ibn Rib'i decided to take on the task. He stepped forward from the circle of men and walked closer to the body of Husayn. With only a few steps he had reached him. Sword in hand, readying himself to take Husayn's life, Shabath stopped in his tracks. Husayn had opened his eyes. As Shabath's eyes met Husayn's, he felt a piercing in his soul. Husayn looked right through him.

Shabath's eyes grew wide. His jaw dropped. He mumbled some words as he dropped his sword and ran away from the scene. "Where are you going, Shabath?!" some of the man called out to him.

He slowed his tracks and looked to the commander's direction and said, "Woe to you, Ibn Saad! You wish to claim innocence from the blood and murder Husayn, while I would be the one responsible for it! I will not meet God with Husayn's blood on my hands!"

Sinan caught up to him and grabbed Shabath. "Damn you, Shabath! I will kill you myself if you do not kill him!"

Unphased by his threat and looking back and forth with a craze in his eyes, Shabath grabbed Sinan and brought him close. "He opened his eyes when I drew near, and they looked like the eyes of the Prophet! Shame did not allow me to kill a man who looked like the Messenger of God. I could not do it, I just could not."

Sinan shoved Shabath to the ground, peering at him with disgust. He looked towards the other men. "Khawli!" He shouted at another man. "Go and sever his head!"

Khawli's feet did not move. He lowered his head. He could not do it. Seeing his hesitation, Sinan cursed him. "May God ruin your arms and sever your hands!"

"Are there any men amongst you to finish him?" Sinan shouted. The response was silence.

"I am more deserving of the honor to kill Husayn than you are. Give me the sword and enough of this nonsense," he said as he grabbed the sword. Sinan knew the gravity of the task. He masked his own hesitation with anger, and took his heavy steps towards Husayn.

As he came closer, Sinan saw the blood that drenched Husayn's body. His eyes were closed. Perhaps he was already dead? Perhaps Sinan did not need to have the burden of killing Husayn? He could claim just enough wickedness for stabbing him, but Sinan did not want to take his last breath. The burden was too great. He took a few more steps to Husayn's bloodied body. His eyes were still closed. Sinan looked around and back at the men. Perhaps he could claim Husayn's life, without actually killing him since he was already dead? But that glimmer of wicked hope died as Husayn opened his eyes.

Sinan looked into Husayn's gleaming eyes and began to tremble. His hands could no longer grasp his sword. Taking steps away from Husayn, without interrupting the trance with Husayn's eyes, Sinan dropped his sword. He did not care to retrieve it.

Sinan scurried away, saying, "I will not have your blood on my hands, I will not have your blood on my hands."

Shimr saw the fleeing Sinan, ran up to him and grabbed him by the collar. "You fool!" Shimr shouted at Sinan. "Why haven't you come with Husayn's head?"

In a hysteria similar to Shabath's, Sinan spoke of Husayn's eyes. "His eyes," Sinan murmured. "His eyes."

"What of his eyes?!" Shimr shook Sinan.

"He opened his eyes when I drew near, he looked right through me. It was as if his father, Ali, was looking at me. His eyes pierced my soul and paralyzed me. I could not dare kill the lion," Sinan said as he looked off in a daze.

"What a coward you are in the midst of battle," Shimr looked at Sinan, disgusted. "Give me the sword, for by God no one is more deserving of Husayn's blood than me. I will kill him whether he is the like of his grandfather Muhammad or his father, Ali!"

The men knew that Shimr was not blowing smoke. Shimr wrapped a veil around his face, exposing only his eyes. "I will finish this," Shimr said, looking at Sinan. "But you are coming with me." He dragged Sinan with him towards Husayn.

As Shimr and Sinan came closer to Husayn, they found him biting on his tongue out of thirst. His state was terrible. It was as if Husayn's flesh did not have an open space for another wound. His greyed beard was drenched in his own blood. Yet his face still glowed with a heavenly light. Seeing Husayn chewing on his tongue out of thirst, Shimr kicked him in his side with his steel boot.

"O son of Ali, do you not claim that your father stands at the Prophet's Pond in Paradise, waiting for you and those he loves? So, stay thirsty until you take a drink from his hand," Shimr mocked Husayn.

Husayn did not respond.

Shimr then looked at Sinan and said, "Sever his head."

"By God, I will not!" Sinan refused with a look of terror in his eyes. "I will not have his grandfather Muhammad be my adversary," Sinan added, as if hoping to be acquitted from the rest of the crimes he had already committed against the Prophet's grandson. Shimr pushed Sinan out of his way and kicked Husayn again. He then sat his knee on the chest of Husayn and kneeled in, speaking into Husayn's ear.

"Do not think I am like the cowards who came to kill you before me," Shimr whispered. "I will slaughter you without batting an eye."

"You have sat on a place that the Prophet used to kiss," Husayn smiled. "Who are you?"

"I am Shimr," he replied under his veil.

"Do you not know who I am?" Husayn asked.

"I know you very well. Your mother is Fatima al-Zahraa, your father is Ali al-Murtada, your grandfather is Muhammad al-Mustafa and your grandmother is Khadija al-Kubra," Shimr replied.

"If you know me, then why would you kill me?"

Shimr replied, "There is a great prize for your head with the new caliph, Yazid."

"Which is more preferable to you, the intercession of my grandfather the Messenger of God or the prize of Yazid?" Husayn offered.

Shimr pressed his knee further into Husayn's chest and replied, "I will take a single coin from the prize of Yazid over intercession from your father and grandfather!"

"Before you kill me," Husayn said. "Lift your mask so that I can see the face of my killer." Shimr smirked with the face of wickedness as he lifted his veil. The man was a leper. He was blind in one eye. His nose was long and protruding like the snout of a dog. His hair was coarse and bristly like that of a pig.

Husayn smiled and looked at the skies above him. "My grandfather has always told the truth."

"And what is it that he said that makes you smile now?" Shimr snarled.

"When I was just a boy, I overheard him speaking to my father," Husayn recalled. "He said, 'Ali, this son of yours will be killed by a leper who is blind in one eye, having a long nose like the snout of a dog and hair like the hair of a pig."

"Does your grandfather liken me to a dog?!" The enraged Shimr grabbed Husayn by the neck. "By God, I will slaughter you from the back as a punishment for your grandfather's words!" Shimr threw Husayn on his face and stabbed him with his dagger twelve times. As Shimr ravaged Husayn's body with his dagger, Husayn called out.

"O Muhammad! O Ali! O Hasan! O Jafar! O Hamza! O Aqeel! O Abbas! I am killed all alone… how distant I am from home." Shimr grabbed Husayn's bloodied beard and slit his throat with his sword. As the blood of Husayn left his body, an angel called from God's throne. "O nation that has become confused, tyrannical, and deviant after its Prophet, may God never bless you with a fast or a day of celebration!"

Shimr then grabbed the head of Husayn and severed it from his body. The damned soldier then hoisted Husayn's head on a long spear and raised it for all to see. Husayn's horse, Dhul-Jinah, stormed the men that surrounded Husayn's body. In those moments, Dhul-Jinah became an army force of his own. The valiant steed knocked the men off their saddles and trampled upon them. In a righteous vengeance, Dhul-Jinah killed a score of Shimr's men. As the men fled from the raging mare, and backed away from Husayn's body, Dhul-Jinah lowered its head and caressed the body of its master. It circled his bloodied corpse and then stained its mane with Husayn's blood.

Dhul-Jinah neighed so loud, the entire battlefield could hear it. The steed then galloped back to the camp of Husayn, where his daughters waited outside for the return of their father. Anxiously waiting, the women's hopeful smiles turned to sorrowful cries as the valiant steed had returned without its knight. The women embraced Husayn's horse and their cries were heard by the heavens.

At the scene of Husayn's body, the murderous men chanted in celebration, while the angels of the heavens wept and wailed with the women and children. The Earth quaked and the sky turned a dark red. As the men chanted God's name celebrating Husayn's beheading, they looked at the skies and grew silent. Fear began to loom in the desert air, as a moment ago the blue sky was pierced with a scorching yellow sun. But now, the sky was darkened by red clouds that rained the blood of martyrs and the tears of the angels. An angel of Heaven called out, filling the skies with his thunderous voice.

> By God, the Imam, and son of an Imam and brother to an Imam, has been killed! The valiant knight, Husayn ibn Ali, has been killed!

A dark dust cloud formed around the men dancing around the head of Husayn. It carried the red sand from the blood of Karbala's martyrs. The men could not see before them, knocking into each other as they tried to escape the sudden desert storm. Nowhere to go and captive to the red dust cloud, the men were sure they were doomed.

"It is God's punishment upon us!" they shouted.

They remained in such a state for what seemed to be an hour, until the storm dissipated. When the storm was gone, the men surrounded the headless body of Husayn once again. Some men decided to count the number of wounds that covered his lifeless body, while others looted and desecrated it without regard. Thirty-three spear lesions, thirty-four sword wounds, and one hundred and twenty arrow wounds were found on Husayn's body. He was fifty-eight years old.

CHAPTER 22

FROM KARBALA TO KUFA

I saw nothing but beauty. It was God's wish that they should be martyred, and they met their deaths valiantly.

– Zaynab bint Ali

They burned their tents. They whipped and tortured the children. They desecrated the bodies of the fallen warriors and stole their belongings. They trampled their bloodied bodies with the hooves of their horses. They rounded up the women and children in ropes and chairs. They severed the heads of the martyrs and placed them on their spears.

The women and the children were made to walk on the hot sands with the severed heads of their loved ones hoisted on spears above them. Ubaydallah had ordered for them to be brough to Kufa so that the people of Kufa could see what happens to those who defy him. Kufa was the city that called Husayn to them. It was the community that invited him to lead them.

The people of Kufa watched as the daughters of Husayn, his women and children, were paraded by the soldiers into the city. They looked on in horror as they saw the heads of Husayn and his companions were hoisted on spears. Women screamed. Children cried. The men took steps back in disbelief. They wailed. They cried. Kufa was in a disarray.

Zaynab did not waste much time before speaking to the people of this city. Her heart was aching at the sight of these people crying now. Now? Now they cry? She stopped outside of the governor's palace where the people had gathered. She did not need a pulpit or a podium. She spoke. Everyone listened. Zaynab's voice filled Kufa.

Praise be to Allah! Blessings be on my grandfather Muhammad and his virtuous progeny!

O people of Kufa! To the deceitful and the treacherous! Do you shed tears? May your tears never dry up and your loud lamentations never cease. You are like the woman that unravels to bits the thread which she has firmly spun. Your faith is nothing but deceit and betrayal. Are there any among you but the immodest, disgraced, vain, spiteful, adulator, enemy and reviler? There are among you those who are as guileful as a beautiful plant growing in filth, or the silver on a grave. Certainly, evil is that which your souls have sent before for you. God is displeased with you and in punishment shall you stay.

Are you wailing and crying? Do cry endlessly and laugh but little, for your deed was so horrendously disgraceful that you will never be able to atone for it. How can you wash away the crime of murdering the grandson of the seal of the prophets, the essence of the message, the master of the youth of paradise, the sanctuary of your nobles, the refuge for whom you resorted during affliction, the bright divine proof of yours, and your master who defended the Prophet's tradition?

What an awful sin you committed! Away with you, for there will be no forgiveness for you today! Certainly, your efforts failed, your hands suffered loss and your bargain is brought to naught. You have made yourselves deserving of the wrath of God. Abasement and humiliation have been brought down upon you.

Woe to you! Do you know how you tore the liver of the Apostle of God? Whom of his womenfolk you exposed? What blood of his you shed? What honor of his you disgraced?

Your deed is most certainly so dangerously ugly and foul that it filled the Earth and sky with its putridness. Are you surprised that it rained blood? The punishment of the Hereafter is infinitely more abasing, and you shall not be helped. Do not make light of the delay of punishment. It is not hastened by the fear of missing the taking of revenge. It will come and surely God is watching.

The people erupted further into a commotion of cries and wails. The soldiers pushed the women and children into the court of Ibn Ziyad. Husayn's severed head was presented to the governor on a platter. He smiled, basking in his victory, and he laughed as Ali ibn Husayn and the children entered. Without any shame, Ibn Ziyad stared at the women. Lady Zaynab tried to veil herself amongst the women. Ibn Ziyad noticed her. He asked who she was. His people told him it was Zaynab bint Ali.

He grinned again and turned towards her. "Praise be to God who disgraced you and revealed you for what you are!"

Zaynab did not hesitate to reply to the tyrant. "All praise be to God who has honored us with His Messenger and purified us from impurity. The one who is disgraced is certainly the degenerate. The one who lies is the lewd. We are not such people. Praise be to God."

Taken aback by her eloquence, Ibn Ziyad paused for a moment, not knowing what to say. Then it came to him. "How did you find what God did to your brother and your family?" Ibn Ziyad snarled. Zaynab's reply would be nothing short of excellence.

I saw nothing but beauty. It was God's wish that they should be martyred, and they met their deaths valiantly. If this was your heart's desire, then you must indeed be content today. But you have killed those whom the Prophet held upon his knee when they were children and whose play filled him with joy. Soon you will stand with them before God and they will demand justice. Beware the Day of Reckoning, O son of Marjana! May your mother be mournful for you.

Ibn Ziyad was getting nervous. He did not expect such strength from a woman, let alone one whose family was just massacred before her eyes. To those who lived in his time, Zaynab most resembled her father, Imam Ali. She spoke just like him. She walked tall like him. Her confidence emanated in everything she said and did, like him. She was her father's daughter.

Trying to save face after being schooled by this immaculate woman, Ibn Ziyad turned to Ali ibn Husayn.

"Who are you?" he demanded.

"I am Ali ibn Husayn," Ali replied.

"Didn't God kill Ali ibn Husayn?" Ibn Ziyad asked.

"I had an older brother. His name was also Ali. He was slain by the people," Ali said firmly.

"It was God who killed him," Ibn Ziyad gritted his teeth.

Ali replied with a verse from the Holy Quran, "God takes the souls at the time of their death" (Quran 39:42).

The governor had lost his patience. "I've had enough. Kill this man now," he ordered his men.

Lady Zaynab jumped in front of Ali and called out to the governor, "Ibn Ziyad! Is it not enough that you have shed all of our blood? You have not spared anyone! If you want to kill him, then you must kill me with him as well."

The crowd that had gathered fell deeper into its wails and cries. "You should know that we are used to being killed. Martyrdom is an honor and a blessing for us," Ali said to the governor.

Ibn Ziyad looked at both of them then said mockingly, "How wonderful is kinship! I think she wants me to kill her with him. Leave him, for I see him now for what he is."

The governor did not give them much time to rest before sending them back on the road to be presented for the next chief to bask in his supposed victory over Husayn. The orphaned caravan of Husayn would be dragged through the unforgiving desert. Ali ibn Husayn, Lady Zaynab, the women and the children were tortured by the whips of Umayyad soldiers. But it was not merely the whips that pained them. Wherever they looked, the pain of the tragedy and captivity was with the orphans of Husayn. When they looked up to the sky, they would see the severed heads of their martyrs hoisted on spears. The Umayyad horsemen paraded the severed heads from town to town, as a proclamation of their victory for the caliphate. When the orphans of Husayn looked down, they saw the chains at their wrists and ankles. They felt the heat of the metal blistering away at their skin. The weight of the sun on their shoulders.

The road was long and unforgiving for the orphans of Husayn. The place they were being taken had a people that did not readily know the family of Husayn for who they were, for the many decades under Muawiya had made the semblance of the Prophet Muhammad a blur. But they would soon be reminded. The truth would gleam like the radiant sun and there is enough light for those who wish to see. Whether they wanted to open their eyes or not, the sun would still shine. The sun of truth would shine its light on *Shaam* – Damascus.

CHAPTER 23

WELCOME TO DAMASCUS

So, scheme whatever you wish to scheme, and carry out your plots, and intensify your efforts. For you will never wipe away our memory, nor will our message fade.

– Zaynab bint Ali

As the daughters of Husayn were brought to the gates of the Umayyad palace, the people of Syria cheered. Paraded as prisoners of war, most thought this was yet another victory for the Muslims against their hostile Byzantine neighbors. They stood outside the gates of the Umayyad palace. The palace was no ordinary structure. It glittered with gems and gold, sparkling under the Syrian sun. Muawiya did not spare any effort in building the most magnificent palace for his son and what would be the Umayyad dynasty to rule for nearly a century. Damascus was their home, and now the capital of the Umayyad caliphate, one they had been building for decades since the rule of the second caliph, Umar.

The family of Husayn waited outside the gates of the palace, surrounded by the Umayyad guards escorting them. The scores of people in celebration continued to shout and yell. An old man came within arm's reach of Ali ibn Husayn and shouted triumphantly in his face.

"Alhamdulillah! Praise be to God! For he has killed you and defeated you! The Almighty has made our leader Yazid victorious over the disbelievers!"

Ali ibn Husayn turned to him and gently asked the old man, "Dear Shaykh, have you read the Holy Quran?"

Annoyed by the question, the old man replied, "Of course I have!"

"Well, have you read the verse, 'Say I do not ask you any reward but the love of the near in kin'?" Ali asked.

"Yes, I have read that verse."

"And have you read verse, 'So give the near of kin their rights'?"

"Yes, I have read that as well," the old man's eyes focused on Ali now with increasing intrigue.

Ali ibn Husayn then asked, "Then have you read the verse, 'Allah only desires to remove all impurity from you O Ahlulbayt and purify you with a perfect purification'?"

"Yes, son, I have read all of that," he replied impatiently.

"Do you know who these verses refer to?" Ali asked.

The old man did not respond.

"It is us. We are the Ahlulbayt whom Allah has purified. We are the near of kin. I am Ali ibn Husayn, the grandson of your Prophet," Ali said. He pointed to the caravan of the chained women and children around him. "We are the sons and daughters of Muhammad."

The old man fell to his knees in disbelief. He grabbed onto the robe of Ali as tears filled his eyes. "Is it truly you?" the old man cried.

"It is us. Without a doubt. It is us."

The man was bewildered and confused. How could the family of the Prophet be brought in chains as prisoners of war before the caliph's palace? Why were the people celebrating? How was he celebrating so ignorantly and foolishly without knowing who these captives truly were? It was much to process. His mind was racing. His heart was thumping so hard it felt like it was going to burst out of his chest.

"Forgive me, O grandson of the Prophet! Please forgive me! What a sin I have committed. Is there repentance for me? Will you forgive me? Will God forgive me?"

"Dear Shaykh, if you repent, God will surely accept your repentance."

The old man prostrated and then raised his head, looking to the heavens. "O Allah! To you I repent, to you I repent. Forgive me and unite me with your Prophet Muhammad and his family!"

As the guards continued to push Ali ibn Husayn and the rest of the captives of the family forward into the courtyard of Yazid's palace, the old man pushed through with them, cursing the name of Yazid. He was quickly removed and disposed of by Yazid's henchmen.

As Yazid sat upon his golden throne, he sipped on his wine and laughed mockingly at Husayn's orphans. They stood before him in the lower level of his courtyard, linked together in chains at their wrists and ankles. The guards finally stopped cracking their whips while in the court of the Umayyad palace as not to agitate the guests of the caliph. The people stared down the women and children, wondering who they were. Their stares were just as piercing as the soldiers' spears. As the women and children struggled to stand in place after the excruciating journey they had endured, Sarjun ibn Mansur walked in and kneeled before Yazid.

"Peace and blessings be upon the Commander of the Faithful," Sarjun greeted the novice caliph.

Yazid replied, annoyed, "Where have you been Sarjun?"

"I was busy writing a poem in honor of your victory sir," Sarjun replied with a wicked smile.

"My victory?" the caliph asked, while knowing the answer.

"Of course, my master. Your victory in this great occasion."

"This is a celebration isn't it!" Yazid replied excitedly, "Go ahead and recite then, Sarjun."

Sarjun gladly took to the center of the court. He threw his robe behind him as he slowly strutted across the marble flooring. Waving and extending his arms emphatically, he recited for all the listening ears, but cared especially for the pair that sat on the throne.

May God protect you, O honored guide
You are the best of rulers and son of the virtuous
You have killed people who only wanted sedition
They cared to cause mischief among the Muslims
Bless your hands O son of Hind
For what you have done to these traitorous people
For you are the Prince of the Faithful
No matter how much your enemy strives
O son of the pure, O son of the virtuous

Slouching back in his glittery throne, Yazid laughed approvingly and took another sip of wine. "I love it! You've done well with this one, Sarjun," Yazid said loudly. His company nodded approvingly with nervous smiles as Yazid gestured to Sarjun to take a seat next to him.

As Yazid's company chuckled and laughed, the women and children were restless. The weight of the chains grew heavier by the minute. Ali ibn Husayn looked at his children, his nieces and nephews, his aunts and cousins, as they were all struggling to stand both against the weight of the chains and the weight of humiliation in the court of the murderous caliph.

"I ask you, Yazid, what would the Prophet say if he saw us in this condition?" Ali ibn Husayn interrupted their jesting mood, "The women and children are still bound in ropes and chains."

Annoyed by the question, Yazid turned to his unassuming son, Muawiya II, who looked visibly uncomfortable with the sight of it all. "What do you think?" Yazid asked his son, who he hoped would be his heir.

Muawiya hesitated but managed to reply, "I do think it would be best to remove their chains, father." Yazid grunted. Scratching his beard, Yazid turned to Sarjun and asked the same.

"It is no harm to remove their chains. Instead, you will be seen as the benevolent leader you are master," Sarjun replied dutifully.

"Fine," Yazid consented with a sigh. Yazid waved down the guard to his right and instructed him coldly. "Remove the prisoners' chains. I will not have them falling over in my court. But bring me the head of Husayn." The guard bowed his head obediently.

As Yazid continued to sip on his wine, staring down the orphans of Husayn, his guard presented Husayn's severed head on a golden platter and placed it before the new caliph. With Husayn's head now before him, Yazid eagerly sat up in his chair. He turned his gaze from the women and children and now focused on the severed head of the Prophet's grandson. He scoffed. Yazid took a cane that lay nearby and began poking at Husayn's head. With every poke, the daughters of Husayn would wail and cry. They saw their father massacred and now his head was being desecrated before their eyes. The more they cried, the more Yazid laughed.

"Aunt Zaynab! Brother Ali! I cannot bear watching this!" the young Fatima shifted and turned as she looked away from Yazid and towards Lady Zaynab and her older brother Ali for consolation.

Ali ibn Husayn held his younger sister as she buried her face into his chest. He looked towards Yazid and raised his voice in the name of God.

"Allahu Akbar! God is great!" Ali began to say as Yazid continued to poke at the head of his father, Husayn. "Beware, O son of Muawiya, whose head you desecrate! My grandfather Ali ibn Abi Talib raised the flag of the Messenger of Allah at Badr, Uhud, and Ahzab, while your grandfather held the flag of the unbelievers!"

At that statement, Yazid stopped and slowly rose out of his seat. With a look of disgust, he shifted towards Ali ibn Husayn. He stood at his throne, breathing heavily, veins bulging from his neck.

"And do you think that I would forget what your grandfathers had done to mine?" Yazid shouted at the son of Husayn. Yazid was regarded by some as a poet himself. In those moments, standing at his throne, he recited a few lines of poetry that manifested the decades of animosity and spite the Umayyads held for the Prophet and his family. Yazid recited.

I wish my forefathers at Badr had witnessed
How the Khazraj are by the thorns annoyed,
They would have been so delighted, saying,
"May your hands, O Yazid, never be paralyzed"
We have killed the masters of their chiefs
That our victory should be equated with Badr,
Indeed, no news from the heavens had come,
Nor was there anything from a god revealed

I will disavow Khandaf if I do not,
Seek revenge from Ahmed's children
For what he, to us, has done.

For a moment, the hall was quiet and Yazid basked in his triumphant glory. But that moment was interrupted by a voice that would echo throughout the ages. The voice of a woman who feared nothing but her Lord. The woman who, when asked of the tragedy she had witnessed, replied that she saw from God, nothing but beauty. Zaynab began her speech in God's praise, like her father Ali and grandfather Muhammad. The crowd turned to her, reminiscing of a time when such praise was heard decades ago with the same sincere voice. The Kufans, who were more familiar with the family of Ali, compared her to her father. "It is as if we are hearing the Commander of the Faithful, Ali, speak to us again." They longed for that sincere voice, a sincerity that had long been lost under the Umayyads, a sincerity that her brother Husayn had lived and died for. To praise the name of Allah, in its truest and purest, for everything belongs to Him and to Him everything returns. Zaynab spoke. All listened.

All praise is due to God, the Lord of the Worlds. May
His blessings be upon His Messenger Muhammad and
his progeny.

True are the words of God, 'Then the end of those who
committed evil was that they disbelieved in God's signs,
and they were ridiculing them.' (Quran 30:10)

*Do you, Yazid, think that when you blocked all the av-
enues of the Earth and the horizons of the heavens before us, so we were driven as captives, that we would be
worthless in the eyes of God, while you would be honored? Or do you think that you enjoy with God such a
great status, so you look down on us? That you become
arrogant and elated when you see the world submissive
to you and things are done as you want them? That you
are where you are, with what is rightfully ours of power
and authority, now in your hands?*

The crowd's eyes continued to grow wide, at a moment's
pause in her speech.

*Wait! Have you forgotten that God has said? 'Do not
regard those who disbelieved that we grant them good
for themselves? We only give them a respite so that they
may increase their sins, and for them there is a humili-
ating torment.' (Quran 3:178)*

*Is it fair, O son of the 'Freed Slaves', that you keep your
ladies and maidens in their chambers under protection,
while you make the daughters of the Prophet captives
with their veils removed and faces exposed? That they
are taken by their enemies from one land to another?
That they are flaunted at watering places and to the
men that man your forts? That their faces are exposed
to all, near or distant, lowly or honorable, having none
of their men with them nor any of their protectors?*

But what can be expected from one descended from those whose mouths chewed the livers of the purified ones and whose flesh grows out of the blood of the martyrs? How can it be expected that one who looks at us begrudgingly with such animosity, would not hate us – the Family of the Prophet? Besides, without any remorse or regard to what you say, you have proudly recited:

'They would have been so delighted, saying,

May your hands, O Yazid, never be paralyzed!'

And now! How dare you hit the lips of Husayn, the Master of the Youths of Paradise? But what would stop you from that, when no compassion remains in your heart? For you have shed the blood of the grandchildren of Muhammad and the stars on earth from among the family of Abd al-Muttalib.

Then you cite your mentors as if you speak to them. Soon you shall be lodged with them. Soon you shall wish you were paralyzed and mute. Soon you shall wish you never said what you said nor did what you did. Soon.

Zaynab then turned her gaze to the heavens and raised her hands in prayer. Those raised, praying hands were reminiscent of her mother Fatima's hands, soon after the death of her own father, the Prophet Muhammad. Fatima prayed against those who oppressed her and her family; Zaynab would do the same. In the name of justice, in the name of faith, in the name of hope, in the name of light.

Dear God, take what belongs to us out of his hands, seek revenge against all those who oppressed us, and let Your wrath descend upon whoever shed our blood and killed our protectors! By God, you have burnt only your own skin, you have cut only your own flesh, and you shall come face to face with the Prophet of God, peace be upon him and his progeny, bearing the burdens of the blood which you have shed, the blood of his offspring, and of his sanctity which you violated, when Allah gathers them together and seeks equity on their behalf.

'And do not reckon those who are slain in the way of Allah as dead. No! They are living with their Lord, receiving their sustenance.' (Quran 3:169)

It is sufficient for us that God is your judge, and that Prophet Muhammad is your enemy. Those who prompted you and those who empowered you to play with the lives of the Muslims will soon know how wretched the end of the oppressors is. You will all find out who will have the most miserable fate and who will be least protected.

Although calamities have forced me to speak to you, you are insignificant in my eyes. Your verbal attacks are great, and your rebuke is too much to bear. The eyes are tearful, and the chests are filled with pain. What is even stranger is that the honored Party of God is being killed by the Party of the 'Freed Ones' – the Party of Satan.

298 | HUSAYN: THE SAGA OF HOPE

Your hands are dripping with our blood and your mouths are feeding on our flesh. The sacred and pure corpses were left as food to the wild beasts of the desert and are sullied by the brutes. If you regard us as your prize of war, you shall soon see us as your opponents – that will be when you find nothing but what your hands had unjustly. 'To God is my complaint, and upon Him do I rely'. (Quran 41:46)

So, scheme whatever you wish to scheme, and carry out your plots, and intensify your efforts. For you will never wipe away our memory, nor will our message fade. You will never exalt to our glory, nor will your shame ever be washed away. Your view shall be proven futile. Your days are limited in number. The call will be made: 'Indeed may the curse of Allah be upon the oppressors...' (Quran 11:18)

All praise is due to God, Lord of the Worlds, who sealed the life of our early ones with happiness and forgiveness, and that of our last ones with martyrdom and mercy. We plead to God to complete His rewards for them, grant them an increase, and recompense us pleasingly. God is the Most Merciful, the Most Compassionate. God suffices us, and He is the Best Guardian.

The people in the audience were moved to tears, though little noise came from them. They listened silently, reflecting, as if revelation was being delivered by this immaculate woman, whose eloquence was simply divine. Though the place bustled with nobles, diplomats, guards, maids, and others, when Zaynab spoke, everything stopped. A pin could be heard if dropped in the palace that day. Even Yazid was captivated. When Zaynab's speech ended, Yazid snapped out of his trance after a moment.

"I have had enough of this!" Yazid turned to one of his hired speakers seated near him. "Go up on the pulpit and speak."

The speaker had one job and one job only. Praise Yazid and his family and curse Husayn and his father Ali. They literally cursed Ali's name in opening sermons of 'religious' gatherings and even Friday congregational prayers. The tradition was inherited from Muawiya's administration. Muawiya had instituted the regular disparaging and cursing of Ali ibn Abi Talib for decades, well before he assumed the caliphate. It was a systematic effort to reshape his people's sentiments towards Ali over the years, and it worked. In its early implementation, some people in Syria opposed it or at least questioned it. Over the years, especially with the increased benefits they enjoyed with the rise of the Umayyads, they were indifferent to it. Many thought it to be in fact part of their faith.

Yazid's speaker walked up to the pulpit. He took a deep breath and began his speech like he always had. "In the name of God, the Beneficent, the Merciful! All thanks are due to God! O people, this is the Commander of the Faithful Yazid ibn Muawiya! He is the best of people and comes from the best of families. He is generous and cares deeply for you. So, obey him and you will win both in this life and the next."

He then turned to the head of Husayn, which was still on a platter in front of Yazid's throne. The speaker looked at it with disgust, pointed at it with disdain, and then looked back at the audience. "Now this is Husayn ibn Ali! Look at him! God has killed him and exposed him for opposing the Commander of the Faithful. Repent to God and leave him or you will lose both in this life and the next. Disown Ali and his family for they have strayed and—"

"Do you see what you have done?" Ali ibn Husayn interrupted Yazid's speaker. "You have bought the pleasure of the creation over the dismay of the Creator, so get yourself ready for your place in Hell." The speaker's eyes widened, and he took a step back from the podium. Ali then turned to Yazid with his head held high and his brow low over his eyes.

"O Yazid, leave me so that I may answer these false claims and speak words that may please God and benefit those who listen."

"Absolutely not!" Yazid replied anxiously.

Yazid's son Muawiya interjected, "Father, let him speak. He may have something good to say. What harm can be done to listen to a few of his words?" Yazid's son was genuinely interested in Ali and indeed anxious to hear what he had to say.

Yazid shot back angrily, "Did you all forget who this man is and what family he belongs to? They are known for their deceiving eloquence, the fathers and their sons. For snakes only give birth to snakes like them."

Sarjun watched Yazid's men, as well as the audience below; they were not convinced. They wanted to hear Ali speak. To shut this down could prove to be even worse. Sarjun turned to Yazid and whispered, "Master, let the young man speak."

Yazid whispered back looking at the crowd, "If he climbs the pulpit, he will only expose me and the Umayyads."

"May his lies be exposed to the people. It is better that you let him be."

Hesitantly, Yazid conceded. "Fine, Ali. You have my permission to speak," Yazid asserted. "But do not make any false statements."

"A person like me never speaks anything but the truth," Ali replied as he gracefully walked up to the pulpit.

All eyes were on the young man who had survived the Massacre of Karbala. He was in his early twenties. He was a father. His son, Muhammad, known as al-Baqir, was three years old. He was being held by one of his aunts. Ali was exhausted, physically and emotionally. The tragedies continued to pile on, day after day, even after witnessing the greatest tragedy of all – the beheading of his father, Husayn. Ali's strength was remarkable, superhuman even. As he gazed at his father's blessed head, he would whisper peace and blessings upon him before he began to speak. Many people did not know who he was, but as he spoke, there no longer was a question in their hearts and minds.

All praise is due to God, for whom there is no beginning. He is the everlasting for whom there is no end. He is the first for whom there is no starting point and the last for whom there is no ending point. He is the one who remains after all beings no longer exist. He measured the nights and the days. He divided them into two parts. So blessed is God, the King, the All-Knowing.

O people, we were given six virtues and we were honored by seven men. We were given knowledge, clemency, leniency, fluency, bravery, and the love for us in the hearts of the faithful. We were honored by the seven who are all from us: the Prophet Muhammad, Jafar al-Tayyar, Hamza – the lion of God and His Prophet, the Commander of the Faithful Ali ibn Abi Talib, the Masters of the Youth of Paradise al-Hasan and al-Husayn, and the Awaited Mahdi, are all from us.

O people, whoever knows me knows me and whoever does not know me, let me tell them who I am and to what family I belong.

O people, I am the son of Mecca and Mina. I am the son of Zamzam and Safa. I am the son of the one who carried the rukn on his mantle. I am the son of the best man who performed the pilgrimage, circulating around the Kaaba and running between Safa and Marwa. I am the son of the one who was transported on the Buraq and was taken by the Angel Gabriel to Sidrat al-Muntaha so he was near his Lord, like the throne of the bow, or even closer. I am the son of the one who led the angels of Heaven in prayers.

O people, I am the son of Ali al-Murtada. I am the son of the one who fought with the messenger of Allah at Badr and Hunayn. I am the son of the one who never disbelieved in God, not even for a blink of an eye. I am the son of the best of the believers and the inheritor of the prophets. I am the son of the commander of the Muslims and the light of those who struggled on God's path. I am the son of the destroyer of God's enemies and those who deviated from the Straight Path. I am the son of the one who scattered the pagans, the most courageous one with the firmest determination. Such is Ali, the father of the grandsons of the prophet – al-Hasan and al-Husayn. That is my grandfather, the prince of the believers, Ali ibn Abi Talib.

O people, I am the son of Fatima al-Zahraa, the best of all women. I am the son of Khadija al-Kubra. And I, yes, I am the son of the one who was slaughtered in Karbala. I am the son of the one whose blood stained its sands. O people, I am the son of the one who was killed unjustly. I am the son of the beheaded one. I am the son of the thirsty one until he passed. I am the son of he whose exposed body lay on the sands for three days. I am the son of he whose head was gifted on a spear. I am the son of the one whose women where captivated and dragged from Karbala to Damascus—

Yazid screamed for his *muadhin*, the caller to prayer, "Where is the muadhin? Where is he? Call for prayer! Call!"

Yazid panicked when he saw the people of his court wailing and crying to the moving words of Ali ibn Husayn. He needed to put an end to this and fast. Ironically, he tried to shut down this moment of spiritual reawakening with the call to prayer. The

muadhin stood beside the pulpit, Ali still standing there, and began the call for prayer.

Allahu Akbar! Allahu Akbar! God is great.

"God is greater, more magnanimous, and more gracious
than what I fear and what I avoid," Ali followed.

Ashhadu an la illah illa Allah. I bear witness that there is no
god but Allah!

"I testify with everyone who testifies that there is no god
besides Him, nor any other lord. My hair, my skin, my body, my
bones, my heart, my mind, and every part of my existence testifies that there is no god but Him." The people were in awe of his
every word. Even the muadhin paused and looked at Ali like he
had never heard anything so profound.

Yazid screamed again at his muadhin, "Call to prayer!"

Ashhadu anna Muhammadan Rasoolullah! I bear witness
that Muhammad is the Messenger of Allah.

Ali then turned to Yazid and said, "O Yazid, this great messenger of God, is he your grandfather or mine? If you say he is
yours, everyone here will know that you are a liar. But if you say
that he is mine, then why did you have my father killed unjustly
and so cruelly? Why did you take his women captive and parade
them in the lands? Brace yourself for the day when you will meet
my grandfather Muhammad as your enemy."

There was chaos in the crowd. The guards tried to keep the
calm, but to no avail. They shouted amongst themselves, and
fights broke out. Confused and scared, Yazid called out, "I did

not kill Husayn! I did not kill Husayn! It was Ubaydallah ibn Ziyad who did it." Some men came up to Ali and kneeled before him in repentance.

"Forgive us, Master Ali. Forgive us, son of God's messenger," they said.

Ali placed his hand on their shoulders and repeated. "May God forgive you, God is the most forgiving." The hope that emanated from Husayn's family was divine. People were baffled by their strength and resolve. No ordinary human being could suffer what they suffered and carry on so.

At the advice of his counsel, Yazid ordered that Ali and his family be taken away at once from his court to prevent further uproar. To the dark dungeons of the Umayyad palace they were sent. Rows of women and children walked down the old staircases. Against heat and cold, their bodies were protected only by the black drapes of clothing they wore, while their hearts were warm with their relentless hope in God's plan.

CHAPTER 24

IN PALACE DUNGEONS

I do not want food. I do not want water. I do not want anything but my father, Husayn!

– Ruqayya bint Husayn

It is said that Husayn's youngest daughter was named Ruqayya. Others have called her Sukayna. She was especially close to her father and so dear to his heart. She was the apple of his eye, and he was her entire world. The aftermath of Ashura was especially difficult for the young daughter of Husayn. She could not quite fathom life after him. Poets would later describe Ruqaya's restlessness in the dungeons of the palace. She tried to sleep like the other children. For a few moments, her eyes would give out to what was hard to discern as a dream.

Ruqayya was in an open green field. The sun radiated above her with its warmth. She ran to her father, Husayn. He embraced her and held her tight. She looked at his big brown eyes and kissed him on his beard. She smiled and laughed. She hugged him again. She did not want to let go. She wanted it to last forever. *I love you, baba.* But the sun suddenly faded away and the field was no longer green. Husayn was gone.

Ruqayya awoke from her dream. She found herself back in the dungeon of the Umayyad palace. She could not go back to sleep, no matter how much she tried. She tossed and turned on the gravel floor that was her bed. Ruqayya was now wide awake. She wanted to see her father again; she just wanted so badly to see his face again. She stared at the cracked ceiling above her and could only see darkness. Ruqayya was only five years old. No matter how young she was, she was not spared from witnessing her father Husayn's killing. She knew he was gone, that she could not be held by him anymore, that she could no longer embrace him and kiss his bearded face. But the young child could not fathom a life without her father. How can there be life without Husayn? There could not. There is not. So, she called out for him, like she always had. Perhaps he would appear this time.

"Father, come back to me. Sukayna cried. Father, I miss you so much. Father Husayn, Father Husayn." She cried these words over and over again.

Some of the other children were also awake, crying for the brothers, uncles, and fathers they lost at Karbala. Other children had fallen asleep in the arms of their aunts. Their bodies ached from the journey. They had grown weak from malnutrition. They were all devastated, exhausted beyond measure. Their bodies were worn down from feeling beaten and humiliated over and over again for weeks on end. How could they not sleep? Ruqayya's eyes remained open and tearful. Though other children lay awake with their own cries, the little Ruqayya's wails were the loudest.

In the upper levels of the palace, Yazid was fast asleep. Under layers of silk blankets and pillows, the Umayyad tyrant's slumber was disrupted by the echoes of children's cries. Irritated, he grunted and called for his guards. Two guards came to Yazid's bedside immediately.

"Yes, master?"

"What is this noise I hear at this time of night?" Yazid's words were slurring as he spoke, half awake.

"The daughters of Husayn are crying, master."

"Well, what do they want?" Yazid replied impatiently.

"His youngest daughter is asking for her father, Husayn. She keeps calling out for him."

"Isn't her father dead? What does she want from a dead man?" Yazid said, almost confused.

"She wants to see him," the guard replied plainly.

"Okay, then let her see her father," Yazid said as he pulled the covers back over his head. The guards looked at each other and understood. They bowed their heads before Yazid as he returned to his slumber. Ruqayya's cries did not subside.

"Where are you, father?" Ruqayya cried. "Where have you gone? Come back to us father! I miss you." Lady Zaynab sat awake beside Ruqayya. She put her arm around her to console her.

"Do not cry, my child," Zaynab told her niece. "I am here for you." But Ruqayya could not be consoled.

"I want to see my father." She repeated. Her older brother Ali ibn Husayn stood at the door of the dungeon cell, watching her and the rest of the children. He saw two guards approaching them now from the outside. One of them held a spear while the other held a platter in both hands. They could not see what was on the platter, other than that it was covered with a piece of cloth. Without saying a word, the guards walked past the women and children and placed the platter on the floor in front of little Ruqayya.

She looked up at them and shook her head. "I do not want food. I do not want water. I do not want anything but my father Husayn!" Ruqayya cried. Zaynab continued to embrace her as she wept. The guards looked at Ali with a look of concern, worry even. As if there was some reluctance in the platter that they brought. Ali understood. The guards walked away and out the doors of the dungeon.

"This is what you asked for, my dear," Ali told his little sister. Ruqayya wiggled out of Zaynab's embrace and sat with her body facing the covered platter. She slowly removed the cloth to see her father's severed head. Ruqayya threw herself onto it and continued to weep. She then caressed his face with her soft little fingers.

> O Father, who did this to you? Who took you away from us? Who dyed your beautiful gray hair with your own blood? Who orphaned me at this young age? Father, I cannot live without you. Life is not worth living without you. Father Husayn, I love you. Father, I miss you. I miss you so much. Please, take me with you. Keep me with you. Father, Husayn.

Ruqayya's cries finally came to an end.

"Aunt Zaynab," Ali uttered as tears filled his eyes. He closed his eyes and the tears fell down his cheeks. Zaynab lifted Ruqayya from Husayn's head. Ruqayya had joined her father. Her little soul could not bear to live any longer. She died of her broken heart. Ali and Zaynab embraced each other as the rest of the women and children cried at the sight of Ruqayya's lifeless body. And still, the journey ahead was long.

CHAPTER 25

BACK TO THE BELOVED

They wanted to hide your grave from your beloved, but they could not.
The sweetness of your soil leads the beloved straight to you.

– Jabir ibn Abdallah al-Ansari

Yazid did not want to keep Husayn's women and children in his palace any longer. He even tried to free himself of blame for the crimes against Husayn and his family. He summoned Ali ibn Husayn and cursed his governor in Kufa.

"May God curse Ibn Marjana!" Yazid shouted. "If I had been with your father, I would have given him everything he asked for and I would have saved him from death, even if I had to sacrifice the life of my own children." Yazid then sighed. "But God decreed what you saw my son," Yazid said as he lowered and shook his head. He waited for a response from Ali, but none came.

"Write to me if you need anything," Yazid continued. "Know that issues will develop with your people, but that you should not join any of them. That would be best."

Ali again did not respond to Yazid. He simply looked away. Thus, he released them to go back home to Medina. The journey back to Medina allowed for two routes: a shorter route directly

284 | HUSAYN: THE SAGA OF HOPE

through Arabia, and a longer route that would bring them back through Karbala. They chose the latter.

In reaching Karbala, the family of Husayn would see a dear old friend of their grandfather's – Jabir ibn Abdallah al-Ansari. Jabir was a companion of the Holy Prophet Muhammad. Jabir was a loyal follower of the Prophet and a deep admirer of his family. The Prophet promised him that he would live a very long life. He asked him to send his peace and blessings upon each of his descendants after the Prophet had passed. He lived to see the Prophet's fifth descendant disciple, Muhammad al-Baqir, the son of Ali ibn Husayn, grow into manhood before Jabir died in 697 AD. But even much before then, after the massacre at Karbala in 680 AD, Jabir was an elderly man.

When he heard of the massacre, he told his servant Atiyya that they would travel to Karbala, even if it was the last thing they would do. Jabir had watched Husayn and his siblings grow up. He was a dear friend to the family ever since he was a young man. Jabir himself grew up on the teachings of the Prophet and in loyalty to Ali and his family. The journey was long and hard on the companion's old body. But they made it. Fate had it that they would arrive at Karbala at the same time as Ali ibn Husayn on their return home to Medina.

"We have reached the land of Karbala, sir!"

Jabir was elated. He had arrived. But sorrow soon took over him as he looked about the arid desert that had soaked the blood of his beloved Muhammad's descendants.

"Atiyya, take me to the river so that I can do my ablution. I wish to visit the grave of my master and the son of my master, Husayn." Atiya helped Jabir along to the Euphrates River. They rolled up their sleeves and took the water in their hands, splashing their faces and washing their arms. Tears rolled down Jabir's cheeks even before he made it to Husayn's grave.

"Peace be upon you, Husayn. Peace be upon you, Husayn." Jabir continued to repeat until Atiyya brought him before Husayn's grave. "Atiya, please take me to the grave of my master Husayn, but let us walk slowly my dear. By God, the Holy Prophet told me that with every step taken in the visit of Husayn, there is a great reward. Peace be upon you, Husayn!"

Atiyya pointed at a few feet ahead of them. "There is the grave of Imam Husayn, sir."

Jabir stopped in his tracks. He nodded with sorrow. "Take me to him my dear, take me to him." His steps were heavy. With each step, yet another tear would fall from Jabir's eyes. He finally arrived at Husayn's grave and his body dropped at its side. He caressed the grave with his hands and spoke from his heart:

They wanted to hide your grave from your beloved, but they could not. The sweetness of your soil leads the beloved straight to you. I find myself now before you, my master Husayn. I am calling your name, but I do not hear your reply. Am I not your beloved? O Husayn, why do you not answer me as I call your blessed name? My longing for you can be compared to none. Master Husayn, please...

Jabir fainted. Atiyya shook him softly to wake him up. He had witnessed this before with Jabir when he first heard of Husayn's martyrdom. The news was too much for him. After a few moments, Jabir again came to consciousness. He continued speaking to his beloved Husayn without skipping a beat.

> *O Husayn, I do not blame you for not answering your beloved. For how can you answer me when they severed your head from your body? How can you answer me when they massacred you so? I bear witness that you are the son of the greatest of God's messengers. You are the son of the Commander of the Faithful. You are the son of a pious progeny and the fifth member of the Prophet's cloak. You are the son of the best of all women. You are the Prince of Paradise. God's peace and blessings be upon you my master, until the Day of Reckoning.*

Jabir lifted his head from the grave and stood up. He gazed at the other graves he could see from afar, graves of the martyrs who fell alongside Husayn on the Day of Ashura. Jabir was sure to visit them and pay his respects to these brave warriors.

"Take me to their graves, Atiyya. To the graves of the champions, the victors, the martyrs who gave their lives for our master Husayn."

As Jabir and Atiyya walked towards the remaining graves of Husayn's companions, Jabir repeated words of salutation, "Peace be upon the victors of God, the victors of Husayn."

"Here are the graves of the martyrs, master Jabir," Atiyya said as he pointed to a small gravesite that had been formed for

the companions who had fallen as martyrs in the Battle of Karbala. Jabir sat at the first grave he saw and spoke aloud, address-
ing all of the fallen warriors.

> *Peace be upon the pure souls that rest in the vicinity of*
> *the Prince of Paradise. Peace be upon the souls that rest*
> *alongside our Master Husayn! To you I send the peace*
> *of God, so long as I live and so long there is day and*
> *there is night. I bear witness, my masters, that we are*
> *with you and share in your great reward! May God's*
> *peace and blessings be upon you, dear companions!*

Atiya was taken aback by that last statement. He turned to
Jabir with an impassioned inquiry.

> *"How could it be that we share in their reward sir?*
> *When we did not strike with a sword nor did our flesh*
> *get pierced by spear or arrow. We did not climb a moun-*
> *tain, nor did we descend into a valley. These martyrs*
> *gave their lives. Their heads were severed from their*
> *bodies. Their children were orphaned, and their wives*
> *were widowed. I do not understand sir."*

Jabir nodded his head, understanding Atiyya's confusion.
He reassured him that his statement did not come from his
whim. Instead, it was from the Prophet himself. Jabir explained,

> *The Messenger of God told me, 'Whoever loves a people*
> *will be resurrected with them and whoever was pleased*
> *by the deeds of the people will be allowed participation*
> *in those deeds.' I swear by the One who sent Muham-*
> *mad as the Prophet of Truth, that my intention to be*

with Husayn and his companions is enough. I cry over that which befell Husayn and his companions, and I join them in their great deed, even though I did not strike with a sword nor did I pierce with an arrow.

Atiyya understood now and embraced Jabir's wisdom. As he nodded in reflection, he looked to the horizon and saw a group of people slowly approaching in the distance.

"Someone is coming," he muttered.

Concerned about who it may be, Jabir told Atiya, "Go and find out who it is quickly, Atiya. But be discreet. If they are Umayyad soldiers, let us hide in a ditch or behind one of these hills." Jabir paused and his face relaxed. "Or it could be Ali ibn Husayn. If it is Ali and his family, then you will be relieved of your services with me, Atiya." Jabir hid behind a boulder while Atiya went to investigate. Some time passed and Jabir looked out from behind the huge rock. He saw Atiya walking alongside the group of people approaching.

"Master Jabir, I come forth with the Imam! Ali ibn Husayn is here. He is here, sir!" Upon hearing that, Jabir stumbled out into view. His legs did not serve how quickly he wanted to walk to the Imam. Ali ibn Husayn rushed to catch him from his fall. Embracing one another, Jabir's eyes teared once again.

"Is that you, Jabir?" Ali said with a smile.

"Yes, my master. I am here." Jabir replied, unable to look up at Ali.

"May God reward you for your visit, dear Jabir."

"Tell me what happened here, O Ali! Tell me, what did you see?" Jabir pleaded. Ali ibn Husayn took a deep breath and sighed. His heart was heavy enough just being back in those lands. But he did not hesitate to tell of what he saw. He would describe the scenes of the battle like they had just happened hours ago. It would be as if Ali yearned to tell the tragedy so that no one would ever forget, so that his father's sacrifice would not be taken for granted, so that the people of his nation would awaken to the truth and that falsehood would be exposed for what it was. Ali told Jabir of what had transpired on that day.

"O Jabir, here is the place where our men were massacred one by one. Here is the place where our tents were set ablaze. Here is where our children were tortured with thirst. Here is the place where our women were dragged and taken captive. If only you could see how my father, Husayn, was in his final hours. He died in the battlefield alone. They tortured him. So many men encircled him, until they all took part in killing him. Until his soul finally departed. Until he died estranged, thirsty, and alone. They severed his head and hoisted it on a spear. They killed the purest of the pure."

Jabir was sobbing uncontrollably. The women and the children nearby cried out Husayn's name. *O Husayn!* They repeated. Jabir wanted to know what happened to the others. He could not help but ask. "Tell me of your brother, Ali al-Akbar. What happened to him? Whenever we missed our beloved Prophet, we looked at him. Surely, the people could not bring themselves to harm him!"

*"My brother fought the noble fight of champions, until
thirst overpowered him. He grew tired by the weight of
his armor and the heat of the sun. My father promised
him a drink with our grandfather Muhammad. The enemies surrounded him and attacked him from behind.
With their spears and their arrows, they cut him to
pieces. My father held him in his arms and cried, 'There
is no life after you O Ali...'"*

Jabir asked about Qasim ibn Hasan. He asked about the
sons of Aqeel and the rest of their cousins. He asked about the
companions, how they fought, and how they died. Ali told of all
that Jabir asked about. He spoke of the companions and how
they chose to stay for Husayn even when he told them they could
leave. He spoke of his brothers and cousins in how they resembled his grandfather Ali in battle, and how they made their father, Husayn, proud. What about *Aba Fadl al-Abbas?* Jabir finally asked. To that question Ali would weep.

*"My uncle was our flagbearer. He was the last to remain
with my father. He wished only to get some water from
the river for the children. But the cursed enemies attacked him. They severed his right arm and then his left.
They showered him with arrows, piercing his chest. The
wicked men struck him on his head from behind and
knocked him off his horse as he tried to ride back to the
camp with the water. He finally called out, 'Peace be
upon you, Brother Husayn!' When his soul departed in
the arms of my father, my father said, 'Now my back is
broken!'"*

Zaynab raised her hands in prayer as she and the children wailed and cried. She was struck with the memories of the Day of Ashura, her last embrace with Abbas, her telling him not to go. Her heart aching as the children cried for water. The last time she saw Abbas as he gallantly rode his horse away from the camp and to the Euphrates.

> *"Peace be upon you my brother Abbas! O Quencher of the Thirsty! Ya Qamar Banu Hashim! You were the moon of our tribe! Peace be upon you brother! And my God's curse be on those who severed your hands and pierced your neck. May they never see His mercy or grace. Peace be upon our protector, our champion, Abbas!"*

Jabir's devastation only grew deeper as he heard Ali and Zaynab recite their tragedy. But he wondered if anyone had remained. There must have been others that were spared.

"Who of your brothers survived? Who remains from the sons of Husayn, master Ali?" Jabir asked sorrowfully.

"Jabir they killed us all. I am the only one to remain. They killed all my brothers, even my baby brother, Abdullah."

"Dear Lord! How did he die? What happened to Abdullah?"

> *"Before my father left the camp for the last time, he saw his son Abdullah who was dying of thirst. He could not nurse and there was no water in our camp. Our uncle Abbas had just been killed. My father took his baby boy and rode into the battlefield. He held him up on his arm and called out to the people. 'O people this child has*

committed no crime. Your issue is with me. Just give
him a sip of water!' The men of the army were split into
two, some who wanted to give Abdullah water and oth-
ers who wanted him to die of thirst. Their commander
ordered his best archer to end the dispute. Harmala
struck my brother with an arrow that pierced his little
throat. His crying finally stopped, as his body stretched
breathless in my father's arms. His blood flowed onto
my father's hands. My father looked to the heavens and
prayed, 'This calamity is made easier knowing that it is
all before your eyes, my Lord.'"

Jabir continued to cry with the rest of Husayn's family, as they remembered Husayn in his final moments. The tragedy continued to be recited over and over again. The story did not become cumbersome or old. They visited the graves. They cried some more. Zaynab and Ali embraced Husayn's orphans. Before sunset, Ali told them they must get back on the road.

"Where are you going, O son of Husayn?" Jabir asked.

"We are going back home, Jabir. Back to the city of our grandfather, the Prophet of God, Muhammad. We are going back to Medina."

Back home they would go, to share the tragedy of Husayn and awaken the conscience of a nation that had gone astray. The massacre at Karbala, and the rest of the crimes of the Umayyads, would be exposed. The story of Husayn would be told by his son Ali and sister Zaynab. Their tragedies would not go in vain. Their sacrifices enlivened the soul of Islam and saved the nation of Muhammad. Through Husayn's blood, his sacrifice, his trag-edy – the religion of God would be saved. Husayn would give light and hope to all. God never left the people, their eyes were simply closed. Husayn's sacrifice opened people's eyes to God's light. Those eyes will always see that light, and feel that love, with the remembrance of Husayn.

Those who read or hear this saga of hope, will be awakened to the love of God that shined through Husayn and his family. Everything Husayn did was for God. We are for God and to Him we shall return. He repeated those words throughout his life and in his final days. It is the ultimate truth and the relentless hope of humanity – God. For that is what Husayn lived and died for. God. Though his tragedy was unbearable and the atrocities com-mitted against him unspeakable, his family carried his message – that love and hope in God – across the ages. With the moun-tain of patience that was Zaynab, and the valley of truth that was Ali, the name of Husayn would echo in eternity.

Husayn. Husayn. Husayn.

SELECT BIBLIOGRAPHY

Abu Mikhnaf, *Maqtal al-Husayn.*

Al-Ameen, Sayyid Muhsin. *Ayan al-Shia* (Beirut: Dar al-Ta'aruf lil-Matboo'at, 1983).

Al-Ameen, Sayyid Muhsin. *Lawa'ij al-Ashjan* (Beirut: Dar al-Ta'aruf lil-Matboo'at, 1983).

Al-Amili, Al-Hur. *Ad-Darul Mamlook.*

Abd Rabbih, Ahmad ibn Muhammad ibn. *al-ʿIqd al-Farīd.* (Beirut: Dār al-Kitāb al-ʿArabī, 1993).

Albodairi, Mohammad Ali. *Understanding Karbala,* abridged and adapted from the original work of Grand Ayatollah Sayyid M.S. al-Hakeem (USA: The Mainstay Foundation, 2017).

Al-Akkad, Abbas Mahmoud. *ʿAbqariyet al-Imam* (Cairo: Nahdet Masr, 2003).

Al-Asfahani, Abu al-Faraj. *Maqātil al-Ṭālibiyyīn* (Beirut: Mu'assisa al-'A'lami li-l-Matbu'at, 1965).

Al-Asfahani, Abu Na'eem. *Hiliyat al-Awliya'* (Cairo: 1932).

Al-ʿAskari, Sayyid Murtadha. *Ahadeeth Umm al-Mu'mineen Aisha* (Beirut: Al-Ghadeer, 1997).

Al-Atheer, Ali Ibn. *Usd al-Ghabah fi Marifat al-Sahabah* (Beirut: Dar Ibn Hazm, 2012).

Al-Atheer, Ali Ibn. *Al-Kamil fi al-Tareekh* (Beirut: Dar al-Kutub al-'Ilmiya, 1987).

Al-Balādhurī, 'Aḥmad ibn Yaḥyā. *Ansab al-Ashraf* (Beirut: Yutlabu Min F. Shataynir, 1978).

Beydoun, Labeeb. *Mawsu'at Karbala* (Beirut, 2007).

Brown, Edward G. A. *Literary History of Persia* (Cambridge: Cambridge University Press, 1919).

Chamseddine, Muhammad Mehdi. *Hussain's Revolution* (USA: The Mainstay Foundation. 2016).

Chamseddine, Muhammad Mehdi. *The Victors of Imam Hussain* (USA: The Mainstay Foundation, 2016).

Chamseddine, Muhammad Mehdi. *The Course of History: A Study in the Peak of Eloquence* (USA: The Mainstay Foundation, 2016).

Chelkowski, Peter J. *Ta'ziyeh: Ritual and Drama in Iran* (New York: New York University Press, 1979)

Goldziher, Ignaz. *Introduction to Islamic Theology and Law* (Princeton: Princeton University Press, 1981).

Al-Hadid, Izz al-Din ibn Abi. *Sharh Nahj al-Balagha*, ed. Muhammad Abu al-Fadl Ibrahim (Cairo: Isa al-Babi al-Halabi, 1959).

Al-Hindi, al-Muttaqi. *Kanz al-Ummal Fee Sunan al-Aqwal wa al-Af'al*, ed. Mahmud Umar al-Dumyati (Beirut: Dār al-Kutub al- 'Ilmīyah, 1998).

Hisham, Abu Muhammad Abdul Malik ibn. *Al-Seerah al-Nabawiyya* (Beirut: Dar al-Ma'rifa, 1982).

Hussein, Taha. *Al-Ftina al-Kubra* (Beirut: Dar al-Ma'aref, 2007).

Ibn Kathir. *Al-Sira Al-Nabawiyyah: The Life of the Prophet Muhammad*, Vol. 1, trans. by Professor Trevor Le Gassick (London: Garnet Publishers, 1998).

Al-Irbilī, 'Alī ibn 'Isā. *Kashf al-Ghumma fī Ma'rifat al-A'imma* (Beirut: Dār al-Adwā', 1985).

Al-Mufid, Shaykh. *Kitab Al-Irshad* (Beirut: Dar al-Mufid, 1993).

Al-Mufid, Shaykh. *Kitab Al-Irshad*, trans. I.K.A. Howard as *The Book of Guidance* (London: The Muhammadi Trust, 1981).

Muir, Sir William. *Annals of the Early Caliphate* (London, 1883).

Al-Muqarram, Sayyid Abd al-Razzaq. *Maqtal al-Husayn*, translated as *Martyrdom Epic of Imam al-Husayn*, trans. Yasin T. al-Jebori (Beirut: Al-Kharsan Foundation for Publications, 2005).

Al-Nesapuri, Al-Hakim. *Al-Mustadrak ala aṣ-Ṣaheeḥayn* (Beirut: Dar al-Ma'rifa, 1970).

Nicholson, Reynold Alleyne. A Literary History of the Arabs (Cambridge: Cambridge University Press 1930).

Al-Qarashi, Baqir Sharif. *The Life of Imam Husayn*, trans. Sayyid Athar Husayn S.H. Rizvi (Qom: Ansariyan Publications, 2010).

Al-Qummi, Shaykh Abbas. *Nafasul Mahmum, Relating to the Heart Rending Tragedy of Karbala*, trans. Aejaz Ali T. Bhujwala (Qom: Ansariyan Publications, 2005).

Al-Shiblanji, Mu'min ibn Hasan. *Nour al-Absar* (Qom: Radi Publishing, 1982).

Al-Tabari, Abu Jafar Muhammad ibn Jarir. *Tareekh al-Rusul wa al-Mulook,* translated as *The History of al-Tabari*, Vol. 15, "The Crisis of the Early Caliphate: The Reign of Uthman, A.D. 644-656/A.H. 24-35", trans. R. Stephen Humphreys (Albany: State University of New York Press, 1990).

Al-Tabari, Abu Jafar Muhammad ibn Jarir. *Tareekh al-Rusul wa al-Mulook,* translated as *The History of al-Tabari*, Vol. 19. "The Community Divided: The Caliphate of Yazid Ibn Muawiyah, trans. I.K.A. Howard (Albany: State University of New York Press, 1991).

Al-Tabari, Abu Jafar Muhammad ibn Jarir. *Tareekh al-Rusul wa al-Mulook,* translated as *The History of al-Tabari*, Vol. 17, "The First Civil War: From the battle of Siffin to the Death of Ali, A.D. 656-661/A.H. 36-40", trans. G.R. Hawting (Albany: State University of New York Press, 1996).

Ibn Ṭāwūs, Sayyid. *Al-Luhūf ala Qatla al-Tufūf,* translated as *The Sighs of Sorrow*, trans. Sayyid Athar Husayn S.H. Rizvi (Qom: Naba Organization, 2015).

Al-Ṭūsī, Shaykh Abi Ja'far. Miṣbāḥ al-*Mutahajjid* (Beirut: Mu'assasat Fiqh al-Shi'a, 1991).

Wellhausen, Julius. *The Arab Kingdom and its Fall*, trans. by Margaret Graham Weir (Calcutta: University of Calcutta, 1927).

www.ingramcontent.com/pod-product-compliance
Lightning Source LLC
Chambersburg PA
CBHW032039090426
42744CB00004B/59